the 2,000 best games & activities

the 2,000 best games & activities

the ultimate guide to raising smart, successful kids

susan kettmann

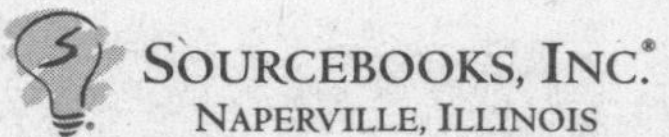

Sourcebooks, Inc.®
Naperville, Illinois

Published by Sourcebooks, Inc.
P.O. Box 4410, Naperville, Illinois 60567-4410
(630) 961-3900
FAX: (630) 961-2168
www.sourcebooks.com

ISBN 1-4022-0414-0 (alk. paper)
Previously categorized by the Library of Congress as:

Kettmann, Susan.
The 2,000 best games and activities / Susan Kettmann.
p. cm.
1. Play. 2. Creative activities and seat work. 3. Early childhood education—Parent participation. I. Title: Two thousand best games and activities. II. Title.
LB1139.35.P55 K48 2004
372.21—dc22

2003023241

Printed and bound in the United States of America
VHG 10 9 8 7 6 5 4 3 2 1

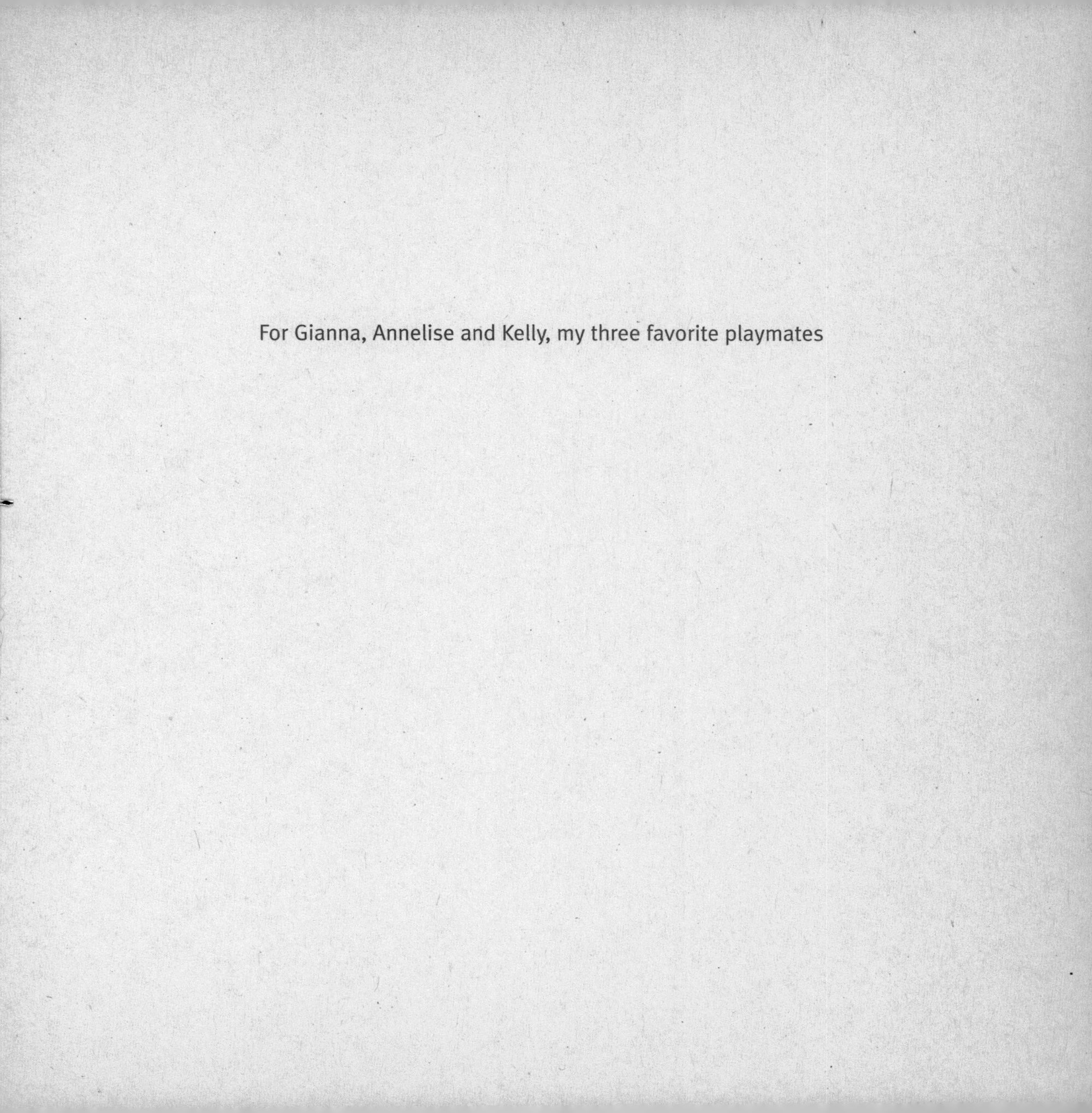

For Gianna, Annelise and Kelly, my three favorite playmates

Table of Contents

1 The Gift of a Lifetime

Children chant the nursery rhyme "Star Light, Star Bright" and blow out birthday candles to make their wishes come true. Such is the innocence of childhood, a time of life when everything is possible. As you read this book, I would ask you to consider the very real possibility that you can make magic happen without resorting to mere wishful thinking. It is absolutely within your power to give the children in your life magnificent gifts that can boost their chances for lifelong happiness and success.

I'm not talking science fiction or wishful thinking. Research in early childhood development is proving that one easy way to boost a child's social, emotional, and intellectual success is to offer the right kinds of play. Considering that a child born today will likely live a hundred years or more, sharing some magic is a good investment of your time.

Children will never learn quite as much and with such mind-altering significance as during their first eight years of life, and you can help to make that time a gift-filled journey. During these years, children's brains are like sponges, eagerly seeking out information and experiences. Play is the biologically programmed activity that stimulates the young child's brain cells, causing complex neural connections to form and resulting in strong memory and thinking skills. In other words, by properly stimulating a child's brain through good play, permanent and lifelong changes take place.

Playing with young children lets you peek into their minds to see how they organize information and approach challenges, and which strengths and weaknesses are forming. Most importantly, the right kinds of play can help you to mold behaviors, letting you influence what you find there. Well-planned play can help you to quiet the active child or embolden the shy one. It can spark a mindset of curiosity and stabilize lifelong habits of good nutrition and physical excellence.

Research is showing us that it isn't enough just to keep children busy. Ensuring optimal development takes more than active hours and attention-getting toys. In fact, the use of play materials labeled *educational* and *developmental* can diminish the most basic element of worthwhile play: a quality adult-child interaction. Toys certainly have their place in play, but they don't guarantee learning, and there is no direct correlation between what children own and what they learn.

Worthwhile play has three components. First, there is *you*, an enthusiastic play companion. You are there to ensure that play teaches as well as entertains. Your willingness to play (and the fact that you have fun at it) tells your child that something important is going on. And the more that you play together, the more you learn about your child, and the easier it becomes to provide good play experiences the next time.

The second ingredient in worthwhile play is *planning*. Of course, you will never want to pass on moments of spontaneous fun when they happen, but if you want to teach important skills, you need a clear idea of how you are going to do that. The activities in this book take care of this aspect of play, making it easy to assemble materials, offer skill-building play activities, and extend the lessons in ways that are fun for both of you.

The third play ingredient is *customizing*. One size does not fit all. Children have unique qualities that influence how they play, and it is important to recognize and respect those personality tendencies. For example, if you have a shy child and you want to help them speak more confidently, an audition in a community play is probably not the best tactic. Building a quiet, pillow-filled corner for whispering secrets might be a better approach.

Customizing play means allowing your child to experience success in ways that are natural and comfortable. Give half a dozen preschool children a lump of dough to play with and you will get six different creations and at least that many ways of producing them. One child will dive in and work furiously without any apparent plan. Another will seek encouragement and direction. A third may watch and copy what the others do. One may even throw it on the floor and walk away. Play shows you how individual children approach tasks, so you can build upon their natural abilities and interests when you set up play.

Although this book is filled with several thousands of fun things to do with children, it is not a play activity book. There are many such books on the market, designed to help keep children busy and happy, and there is nothing wrong with that goal.

Rather, this book is more of a skill-building guide. It offers you a chance to organize your play around seven critical skill areas so that you can begin to recognize and reinforce behaviors that are important to you and to each child you play with. The seven skill areas were chosen because they are important to school and social success with peers and adults.

Using this book can help you maximize the time you spend with children by creating successful play experiences that accomplish meaningful growth. By focusing on one or several of the skill areas offered, you can begin to make substantive changes in your child's capacities and abilities. In the next chapter, we will explore the seven chosen skill areas and look at concrete ways to begin having fun with the children you love while guiding them toward successful development.

Seven Skills to Build On

Children play from the moment they open their eyes until the moment they fall asleep at night. And who is to say that they aren't playing in their dreams, as well? We were all children once and when we were, we played. My, how we played. We played with neighborhood friends and with our few favorite toys, sometimes until they fell apart. We lived for birthdays, holidays, and the endless days of summer vacation. We played in tree houses, under blanket-draped tables, and in imaginary places in our minds. Play made the days long, the weeks endless, and the years seem like perpetual chunks of time.

This book is about using play, that most natural of childhood activities, to systematically pass on valuable life skills. It is also about keeping unnecessary or inappropriate commercialism out of play and focusing on the adult-child interaction that is critical to learning. In spite of the battle waged by the toy industry to convince us otherwise, the fact remains that we can give children a boost in life without spending money, as long as we are spending time.

This book focuses on seven critical skill areas: *Communication, Concentration, Curiosity, Decision Making, Kindness, Physical Ability* and *Playfulness*. Of course there are dozens of other worthwhile things to teach children, but these seven were chosen for their value in promoting school readiness and lifelong success. Once you become familiar with recognizing and setting up skill-building play, you can easily branch out into other areas of competence that are important to you.

The seven skills are presented in alphabetical order, not in order of importance. That means that you don't need to read the whole book before you start playing. You can begin anywhere, focusing on one skill or on several, remembering that children, like adults, can acquire multiple skills at the same time. If you work with skills that are meaningful to you, you will enjoy the results even more as you see, firsthand, the immediate benefits of your time and love.

Each skill is presented in its own chapter along with hundreds of play activities that provide direct experiences with the skill concept. The activities are arranged chronologically under the general age-related headings: *Babies, Toddlers, Three Years, Four Years*, and *Kindergarten through Grade Three.* Each activity lists the supplies you will need and the approximate amount of time you can expect your child to remain engaged in the activity.

Also, the activities suggest *Extensions*, which are changes to the activity that can stimulate further involvement in the activity when interest begins to wane. The changes are slight but frequently offer just enough novelty to keep things going, thereby reinforcing the lessons that can then be learned that much more.

The activities in this book were collected during my more than twenty years working with young children in educational and day-care settings as a child development specialist. In other words, each of them has been thoroughly kid-tested. This should put your mind at ease if you are a little nervous about being a playmate again.

Some activities will appeal more to one child than to another, and paying attention to those preferences will help you plan better play each time. It is also good to remember that young children, even when they are having fun, need positive adult reinforcement to help them measure their progress. You can help your child believe that she is a creative artist, a fast runner, and a spellbinding communicator, and you do this by paying attention and joining in the fun.

Becoming a good playmate is easy. Children love to play with the adults they love and will rarely refuse your involvement and companionship. When leaving my granddaughter recently after nearly ten hours of non-stop play, she grabbed me by the legs and begged me not to leave because we hadn't played enough—such sweet words to my ears. Sweet words of success.

As you, too, become the instigator of play that is both entertaining and purposeful, you will hear giggles of joy while watching self-esteem soar and valuable skills take root. And because the fun of playing with children is so contagious, the more you do it, the more playful you will become along the way, regaining those lost moments from your own childhood and building relationships that will last a lifetime.

3 How to Use This Book

This book is easy to use. Whether you are a parent and daily companion or an occasionally visiting relative, you can use it to play successfully and experience meaningful adult-child interactions without any special training and without spending a lot of money. This is not primarily an activity book, although that is one of its features. Rather, it is a guide to playing with a focus on the process and experience so that your child learns valuable skills.

Be sure to assemble all the required materials as they are listed for each activity ahead of time so you can focus on the play and minimize distractions or interruptions. Giving your child your full attention sends a strong message about the value and importance of your time together.

After you choose a skill area, scan through to find the section that most closely matches the age of your child. Ages are provided to give you general guidance about the appropriate level of challenge. If play is too easy or too difficult, your child will lose interest, so you will have to experiment each time you get started. Children frequently enjoy activities on either side of their age range. Experiment with the activities that sound fun to you or that you think will interest your child, but be willing to switch courses whenever necessary. It is also a good idea to alternate quiet activities with active ones to keep an overall balance.

There is a time suggested for each activity. It is an estimate of the likely duration of interest that you can expect, made based on watching a wide range of children. I have assigned these cautiously, and it is likely you will exceed these limits in your play sometimes. Take cues from your child's level of interest and enjoyment and use the time designation to plan for a series of activities that match the time you have available to play so you don't run out of things to do. Good planning can keep your playtime lively and energized.

Most of the activities in this book use common household items and can be done without ever walking into a toy store. Occasionally, you will find a "$" next to a listed material. That means that you may need to buy it, but it will probably be inexpensive. Paints, felt pens, glitter, and tissue paper are examples of items that are listed with the "$" mark.

I am assuming that households with young children have at least some story books, crayons, dolls, stuffed animals, and office supplies like tape, glue, and paper. (See Appendix B for a list of time-tested, durable, and low-cost toys to buy should you ever decide to venture into the marketplace.)

Finally, as stated in the previous chapter, most activities offer additional suggestions called *Extensions*. The attention span of the young child is predictably short—anywhere from a minute or two for babies to some twenty or thirty minutes for young children. The Extensions are designed to keep the play going when you are enjoying an activity but the interest is winding down. By introducing a slight variation in the equipment or directions, you can often make a good play experience even better.

This book is about spending time with children, for you are the key ingredient in purposeful play. It isn't about spending *more* time with children, although that is certainly a worthwhile goal. Rather, it is about spending time in meaningful ways. Even a bare minimum of time spent in quality, goal-oriented play with a grandparent or relative who can only visit once a year can produce powerful results if it is well-planned and thoughtfully executed.

Using this book can help you become a competent playmate if you trust your instincts, think back to your own childhood, and refuse to be enticed into buying play equipment that you don't need. When you focus on children at their current developmental stages, you will be able to help them to meet their mental, emotional, physical, and social challenges, and you will have a great deal of fun along the way.

The Ages and Stages of Play

Baby Play

Current research offers us fascinating insights into the world of babies. No longer do we consider them to be helpless and thoughtless. We now know that even before birth every nerve cell has formed and is in place, ready to make learning connections. You can help connections form by offering well-planned and stimulating play: things like taking your baby in your arms to talk, to read, or even just to stare into each other's eyes.

Instead of providing an atmosphere of quiet and rest, we now know that a certain amount of thoughtful stimulation and activity is good right from the start. Babies only a few days old can distinguish visual patterns, human faces, and light from dark. They can also identify Mom by smell from across the room. Babies are designed to interact and learn, so we can enjoy playing right from the start.

Most charming of all is the fact that babies talk, move, and learn in individual ways. Some babies make frequent and early verbal advances while others focus on what is going on by watching quietly, charming us with their bright eyes and wonderful smiles. Some babies want to be talked to, others to be handled continually, and still others left alone to gaze and observe on their own. Some babies demand attention, and others take things in stride. Some are easily startled, and others thrive in the midst of activity and noise.

Personalities are present from the start, providing clues that can help you use the activities in this book to full advantage, meeting your child's unique needs with respect and informed attention.

Babies play to gather basic information about the world around them, to grow stronger physically, and to build attachments to the significant people in their lives. They are top-notch explorers who will touch and taste everything within reach, beginning with parts of their own bodies and progressing into the environment as their ability to get around improves. In the first year, they will master the highly complex physical feats of moving and balance, by learning to turn over, sit up, crawl, and pull the entire body upright, in that order. To assist them with these developmental tasks, you can keep the following baby play goals in mind:

Play Task 1: Learn about your baby's preferred interaction style.

There is no single right style to interact with others, and if you avoid making comparisons to other babies, you will be better able to observe your own child impartially and appreciate the individuality. Take cues from your baby's comfort zone and ask yourself these questions as you observe:

- Is my baby confident, timid, or a little reckless?
- Is my baby more likely to observe, seek help, or act independently?
- Does my baby seek stimulation or prefer a quiet environment?

Play Task 2: Provide an environment rich with stimulation.

Babies learn best by seeing, hearing, and touching. The mouth plays an important role in the exploration of just about everything. As you prepare a rich and stimulating environment for your baby, ask yourself these questions:

- Does my baby hear a variety of household sounds, including music and talking?
- Are there other people around to watch, if my baby can't move about yet?
- Is my baby moved from one spot to another occasionally so the surroundings and scenery change?

- Are there objects to look at near my baby's eye level?

Play Task 3: Help your baby to develop coping skills by limiting delays and frustrations and by moderating stimulation.

Babies should not be left to cry for prolonged periods of time or to become overly hungry or tired. Anticipating needs is the most effective way to deal with your baby's unrefined coping skills as you ask yourself these questions:

- Can I help my baby persevere sometimes in trying to reach for a toy?
- When my baby's needs have been met, can she play alone for a few minutes with me nearby?
- Do I respond quickly to signs of hunger and fatigue when they are communicated?

Toddler Play

Best known for their headstrong and demanding behaviors, toddlers provide us with clear indications of personality traits if we can stand back and be patient enough to appreciate them. Toddlers have limited coping abilities, and their needs are immediate and strong. They can be stubborn and are apt to have at least occasional temper tantrums. Taken in stride and in the larger developmental context, challenging behaviors are balanced by an abundance of affection and joy in this age of exploration and continual discovery.

Toddlers love being touched and hugged, with some demanding a high level of physical attention while others seek it out mainly when they feel threatened, tired, or insecure. Their main developmental tasks are movement and language. There is great progress from scooting to standing, toddling, and ultimately moving at top speed on two feet. The world looks quite different from an upright position, and everything within reach becomes fair game. Lacking a developed memory, toddlers can't remember what you just told them, even though they might understand what you are saying at a given moment, making discipline and rules less of realistic focus. Words are also forming along with enchanting expression and inflection, which makes toddlers sound quite grown-up sometimes.

As we play, we need to take all of these factors into consideration, along with the reality of very short attention spans and a love of novelty and stimulation.

Play Task 1: Help your toddler express preferences by repeating play experiences that they enjoy.

Toddlers love repetition and familiar favorites. A beloved doll or a familiar storybook never gets old and the seemingly inane activity of filling and dumping is a favorite. Boxes, purses, and anything else that can be filled up and emptied just for the fun of it over and over again never go out of style. Toddlers can't get too much of a good thing, and as you play with them, ask yourself these questions:

- What activities does my toddler like to do best?
- Is repetition of those favorites built into each day?
- Is there time for silly play, like bouncing and singing songs?

Play Task 2: Provide as much safe exploration as possible.

Your toddler wants free reign of the house, so safety needs to be constantly on your mind. Arrange a few cupboards and boxes, filled with your toddler's favorite possessions. Make sure to take your toddler outdoors to explore as often as possible, too. When planning for exploration anywhere, ask yourself these questions:

- What is at my toddler's eye level?
- Is the environment safe from that point of view? (You may need to get down and see for yourself.)
- Is the play environment enticing and changing regularly with the addition and removal of items to play with?
- Are there places where my child's favorite toys are stored so they can be reached without my help?

Play Task 3: Provide an available lap whenever your toddler needs it.

Play behaviors are still unpredictable, and toddlers can become over-stimulated, tired, and frightened without warning. A short time in a friendly lap can usually restore the equilibrium, and then you can send them back into happy play. Taking this into account, ask yourself these questions:

- How often does my toddler need to be held and reassured?

- Are there predictable times during the day or certain events that don't seem to go well?
- Do I plan quiet activities to alternate with active ones so my toddler isn't overstimulated?

Preschool Play (Ages Three and Four)

Fingers replace mouths as the primary tool of exploration, and toys are most fun when they can be handled and manipulated, or even disassembled and put back together. During these years, your child is learning the basics of physics through the handling of materials like water, sand, blocks, wheeled toys, and puzzles. There is a growing fascination with how things work, weigh, and feel to the touch. You will often hear the words *how* and *why*.

This is an active stage, with your child climbing higher, moving faster, and pushing the limits that you have established for safety. Keep in mind that preschoolers believe they are invincible. You should supervise their play closely without seeming overprotective or alarmed by their bravado.

If you encourage your child, running, climbing, and jumping will be mastered through vigorous play at the playground and in the yard. Eye-hand coordination is challenged through drawing recognizable pictures, piecing together 20- to 30-piece puzzles, stringing beads, and planting gardens. Your child will enjoy experimenting with art materials, paint, and coloring tools, and, of course, stories and books that require imagination and thought.

Waiting, sharing, and taking turns are still difficult, although not impossible in small doses. Imagination grows and brings on the first onslaught of nightmares about monsters and other horrible creatures. There is improved memory and generally a desire to please adults.

Play begins to take on an element of group activity now, although shy children will prefer playing near, but not necessarily interacting with, other children. Preschoolers are also learning to use words instead of shoving, hitting, or crying to get their way.

Play Task 1: Expose your preschooler to peer play for practice with basic social skills.

It is important now for your child to have access to playgrounds, preschool, or other group settings where physical and social challenges will happen naturally. Try not to interfere more than necessary in their awkward attempts to play with others. Be sure to ask yourself these questions as you move your child out into the world:

- Does my child get the vigorous exercise needed to assure that proper muscle and bone development can take place?
- Is my child exposed to early sports skills like throwing and kicking?
- How about jumping and climbing?
- Is time in front of the television limited so that adequate exercise can take place?
- Can my child play next to and with other children of the same age without too much conflict?
- Does my child have opportunities to give and receive directions from peers?

Play Task 2: Provide ample opportunities to use the fingers for small motor tasks.

You can have your child string beads and other small objects, color and draw simple pictures, build with small table blocks, and mold clay or dough. When assessing fine-motor-skill development, ask yourself these questions:

- Are my child's fingers gaining strength through small motor activities in order to prepare for emerging drawing and writing tasks?
- Do we have fun creating pictures and stories together?
- Are art materials like pens, crayons, and paper available without my child having to ask for them?

Play Task 3: Encourage pretend play and the use of imagination by joining in the fun.

Make believe you are hunting while you are at the grocery store, flying to the moon while you are stuck in traffic, or exploring a dark jungle while you visit parks and walk around the neighborhood. While you are pretending together, ask yourself these questions regarding imaginative play:

- Do I make sure to initiate pretend play regularly and to give it my whole attention?
- Do I offer stories and books that require imagination?
- Do I limit time in front of the television where visual images negate creative thinking?
- Do I encourage doll and puppet play to help my child express difficult feelings?

Kindergarten through Grade Three

Gone are pudgy cheeks and protruding tummies. In their place you find gangly limbs, bruised knees, and a quest for independence from your control. There is a push to explore, try out, and test limits. The worldview of these children is considerably expanded, and they will insist on a stake in their own control and on doing things for themselves. Play is a safe way to accomplish this end and to help them begin to let go of your prior total adult authority.

Play with friends is very important, although school children are also very interested in what you do with your time. They want to please the important adults in their lives and will enjoy having small tasks and responsibilities in their routines, as well as trying out adult tools and being guided into learning adult tasks like cooking and gardening.

The mastery of more advanced motor skills begins, and that makes your assistance critical so they can learn correctly. Throwing, catching, shooting baskets, jumping rope, and riding bikes are all favorite activities that enhance self-esteem with peers. Competitiveness is at a high level, but these eager learners can become easily frustrated as they discover the work and time entailed in mastering such skills.

Play that challenges children to problem solve and come up with new ways of doing things and play that involves adult tools instead of child-sized ones are sure to be hits. School children like many of the same things that preschoolers do, but with some level of added complexity and skill challenge.

Play Task 1: Provide basic equipment and time to help school children master sports and ball skills.

Proper throwing techniques are learned at this stage, as well as skills like batting, target shooting, balancing, bike riding, and skating. These are also good years to work on developing adequate swimming skills. When looking at this important physical development area, ask yourself these questions:

- When an interest is shown in a sports or physical activity, do I genuinely encourage it?
- Does my child spend more time outdoors than inside at sedentary activities?
- Does my child help to develop rules for around the house and when playing with other children?
- Do I guide his interest in some of my adult hobbies or sports?

Play Task 2: Involve school children in real-life projects like home chores, gardening, and simple hobby and building projects.

Try to resist the urge to teach everything, and challenge your child to make suggestions, solve simple problems, and try alternate solutions, even if that means they fail sometimes. To help with this task, ask yourself these questions:

- Do I encourage participation in regular household chores in positive ways?
- Is my child learning to do long-term projects spread out over time, like planting a garden or painting a picture?
- Do I ask my child for advice or directions sometimes to enhance their self-confidence?

Play Task 3: Ask for your child's opinions and challenge her growing reasoning abilities, always answering her questions as honestly as possible.

Your child's reasoning ability improves with age, and you can carry on interesting and helpful conversations if you treat your child as an equal and respect her emerging thought patterns. To guide your actions in this area, ask yourself these questions:

- What have I learned from my child recently?
- Who are her best friends?
- What is her favorite food?
- What is her favorite activity in school and at home?

communication 5

Language is a thrilling dance that must be done in tandem. During the early childhood years, vocabularies grow so quickly that by age three or four, children know several thousand words. Grammar, tense, and syntax also develop from listening and practicing. To help children communicate well we must soak them in a language-rich environment and invite them to play in it with us in ways that are sometimes serious and sometimes silly.

You can support your child's skills in this area by paying attention to what is said and by showing genuine interest in his ideas and questions. Putting feelings into words is a difficult task and children need to practice collecting their thoughts and expressing them effectively. Young children know a great deal more than they can put into words and are easily frustrated in trying to do so. It is often easier for us to anticipate children's needs and frame their thoughts for them so that all they have to do is nod *yes* or *no*, but that does them a disservice. Communication skills are learned through trial and error, through patience and listening.

It is important to acknowledge that part of communication is inborn and relates to a child's personality. Some children naturally prefer to watch and listen while others want to be in the center of the conversation, or even leading it. Expecting to turn your quiet or shy child into an orator is probably unrealistic, although you can work to assure a maximized potential in expressiveness. It is also unfair to cut off the talkative child who is doing what comes naturally and hasn't learned social conventions for shared conversations.

When we listen, children delight us with their fresh observations. A two-minute walk to the corner takes twenty as we explore each bug, twig, and crack in the sidewalk. When we share conversations, we share the world on a whole new level.

The activities in this chapter provide deliberate and fun ideas to promote the kind of camaraderie that spurs good communication. They are also varied enough to respect individual personality and style. When you choose a hands-on exploration of basic materials like water, dirt and sand, words will flow naturally about what is seen and felt. When you opt for imaginary and pretend activities, you open the door for the expression of abstract thoughts and emotions about wishes and fears. When it comes to sharing ideas, there are no limits to the surprises in store for you.

Best of all, the following activities promote the dance of language that will bring you closer and closer to the essence of each special and unique child.

Almost Words

Time: 5 to 10 minutes

Materials: None

If you've been cooing and babbling to your baby, "almost" words will emerge in the second half of the first year, usually consisting of a simple repeated syllable, such as *mama, baba,* or *dada*. Repeat these sounds often to show your baby that you hear and delight in them.

Extension:

- Repeat the syllables and then use the correct word in a sentence, such as, "You want Daddy to play with you?" or, "Are you hungry for your bottle?"

Box Talk

Time: 5 to 10 minutes

Materials: Small box that can be held in your hand

It will interest your baby if you put the box up to your mouth and talk into it like a telephone while you sit close together. Talk to your baby since your voice will have a slight echo.

Extensions:

- Use different boxes and different voices.
- Put the box up to the baby's mouth and encourage babbling.
- Use 2 boxes and encourage the baby to talk back to you.
- A toy telephone ($) is always a popular item for babies who are experimenting with the voice.

Buzzy Bee

Time: 5 to 10 minutes

Materials: None

Communications can be fun when they are silly. While holding your baby on your lap, move your fingers around in the air and make a buzzing sound. Make the *buzzy bee* land on your baby's tummy with a tickle. Repeat for as long as your baby is interested.

Extensions:

- Make the bee stop dramatically and then suddenly go again.
- At mealtime, pretend to let the bee eat some of the food.
- Make other sounds with your mouth as you draw the baby toward your face.

Can You Hear Me?

Time: 5 to 10 minutes

Materials: Large pieces of furniture to hide behind

In this variation of peekaboo, you hide behind a piece of furniture and call your baby by name, grabbing their attention before you pop out.

Extensions:

- Play this game by calling from a nearby room.
- Play this game using a large bath towel to cover your head.
- Peek out from the side of your baby's bed after naptime.

Early Conversations

Time: 5 to 10 minutes

Materials: None

Babies are fascinated with faces and voices, and your first communications are through the sounds you make and the nearness of your face. It doesn't matter what you say, as long as you are up close and personal, so chatter away.

Extensions:

- Take the baby's hand and run it gently over your mouth, hair, eyes, and nose, talking about what you are doing.
- Repeat, using your hand on the baby's face.
- Watch carefully and repeat any sounds the baby makes, responding enthusiastically with your attention, smiles, and laughter.
- Bounce the baby to the rhythm of your words, particularly as you repeat phrases and sounds.
- Use nursery rhymes as you play. They have a rhythm and cadence that children have loved for hundreds of years.

Fun with Faces

Time: 5 to 10 minutes

Materials: None

It is always fun for your baby to explore your face. Put your baby's hand on one part of your face or head, such as your nose, mouth, chin, ear, etc. and say what it is.

Extensions:

- Take turns going back and forth between the baby's body parts and yours. Talk about what you are doing.
- Use a stuffed animal or doll to point to body parts.

Greetings

Time: 5 minutes

Materials: None

You can help your baby understand that people are fun by greeting folks wherever you go.

Extensions:

- Always greet your baby by name after naps and in the morning.
- Include store clerks, other shoppers, and people who are out and about in your greetings.
- Greet each other in front of a mirror.
- When a family member or friend comes in the room, pick up the baby and say, "Look who's here!"

Hide and Find

Time: 5 to 10 minutes

Materials: Towel or small blanket

This activity helps your baby learn that people and objects go away and come back. Pop out unexpectedly from behind the cloth saying, "Peekaboo!" to the surprised giggles of your baby.

Extensions:

- Play this game by popping out from behind furniture.
- Reverse the roles by putting the towel over the baby's head.
- Put a toy under the towel and ask the baby where it went and when it is coming back. Then have it pop out.

In and Out

Time: 5 to 10 minutes

Materials: Medium-sized box or laundry basket, familiar objects or toys

Once your baby can sit up, there is much to be learned from the simple act of filling and emptying just about anything. Place objects into a box or laundry basket and demonstrate how to take them out and put them back in, talking about what you are doing as you work together.

Extensions:

- You can make it even more fun by using a silly voice and making the objects run and jump into the laundry basket.
- Name each toy as it goes in and out.
- Hide the toys behind you and take them out one at a time, saying, "Oh, here's the little kitten (ball, book...)." Hand each one to your baby to put into the basket.
- Help your baby gather more objects to put in and take out. Talk about what you are looking for and doing with them.

Pointing Power

Time: 5 to 10 minutes

Materials: None

Everything has a name, and it is fun to hear the words. Teach your baby to point at objects so you can say what they are. It will quickly become a game to your baby.

Extensions:

- Reverse the game by asking, "What's that?" as you point to objects.
- Play this game in the car as you look out the windows.

Scribbles

Time: 5 to 10 minutes

Materials: Large writing tools such as felt pens ($), different kinds of paper (paper bags, butcher, computer), masking tape

Scribbling is the first stage in writing and its purpose is to build hand and finger strength. Tape the paper to the highchair tray or a tabletop and put the drawing tools in your baby's hand, demonstrating how to scribble. Part of the communication will be to help your baby learn not to put them into his mouth. Try saying, "No, we don't eat these. We color on the paper."

Extensions:

- Hold the baby in your lap and color together on a clipboard or paper pad.
- Hang some of the scribbles in a prominent place and point them out to others while the baby is nearby.
- Tape a large piece of paper to a flat surface outdoors and scribble together.
- Use chalk ($) to scribble on everything outside.
- A carefully supervised white board with pens ($) makes scribbling easy for little hands.
- Over-sized crayons make a nice addition to a baby's art supplies.

Talk to Me

Time: 5 minutes

Materials: None

You can use routines like diapering and dressing to make your baby feel included. Talk about what you are doing as you slip on the shirt or pants, saying things like, "We're going to put on your pants now," or, "Here goes your arm." Your baby will look forward to these intimate conversations and the growing bond between you.

Extensions:

- When your baby is used to hearing about what you are doing, the next step is to ask permission and then say, "Thank you."
- When your baby wakes up, show how happy you are to be back together by saying something like, "I missed you, and now we can play."

Tell Me about It

Time: 5 to 10 minutes

Materials: None

Babies love the cadence of language and will enjoy sitting on your lap while you ask questions with a clear inflection at the end of each sentence. You will probably get back a few giggles and some eye contact, body language, and babbling or cooing.

Extensions:

- Initiate conversation when you are traveling in the car and cannot touch.
- Include the baby in conversations at dinner with the rest of the family.

Touch and Learn

Time: 5 to 10 minutes

Materials: Common household objects without corners or sharp edges

Part of baby's work is to learn about all of the things around the house, and one way to encourage your infant is to touch. As you move about the house, say the names of familiar objects and delight as the little fingers explore the things to which you bring attention.

Extensions:

- Take a soft object (stuffed animals work well) and as you say what it is, nuzzle it into the baby's tummy.
- Put some small objects into a basket and say what they are as the baby removes them: "That's a ball. Show me the ball."
- Point out common objects when you are out shopping or traveling.
- Hold the baby and look out the window together, talking about what you see.

Wiggly Tongue

Time: 5 to 10 minutes

Materials: None

The tongue is such a fun and important talking tool. While holding the baby on your lap, stick out your tongue and move it around until your baby touches it.

Extensions:

- Move your tongue up and down and side to side, watching the baby's reactions closely.
- Touch the baby's tongue as you are moving and drawing attention to your own.
- Take the baby in front of a mirror and do these tongue games together.
- Make a "raspberry" noise with your tongue, encouraging the baby to copy you.

Calm Down

Time: 5 to 10 minutes

Materials: None

To get your child to listen to you, get down on their eye level and speak slowly while making eye contact. Keep what you have to say simple and short.

Extensions:

- The next time you are shopping and see a child fussing about something, talk quietly to your child about her behavior.
- Practice making eye contact with your child by a silly game of staring into each other's eyes.

Dirty Vegetables

Time: 5 to 10 minutes

Materials: Vegetables such as carrots or potatoes, scrub brush

Scoot your child up to the sink on a chair or step stool and demonstrate how to use the brush to clean the vegetables. Talk about how vegetables grow and why we wash them.

Extensions:

- Cook, clean, and eat vegetables together.
- Visit a garden or grow some root vegetables (carrots or radishes are quick and easy) that can be pulled out of the ground, dirt and all.
- Take a few vegetables into the bathtub for cleaning during bath time.

Finger Walk

Time: 10 to 15 minutes

Materials: Book with pictures

Open a familiar book and pick out an object on the page. Say, "I see a...." Walk your fingers around the page until you come to it and shout, "Here it is!"

Extensions:

- Go back through the book and let the child walk fingers through the pages and say the words.
- Walk your fingers together through the book.

First Pretending

Time: 5 to 10 minutes

Materials: 3 hats of any kind

The hats can help you to introduce pretend play if you change your mood and voice with each hat. Put on a hat and act silly. Place the hat on the child's head and repeat.

Extensions:

- Hand the hat to the child to put on without your help.
- Move this activity in front of a mirror.
- Play peekaboo from behind a hat.
- Line up some dolls or stuffed animals and put the hats on them.

Gab About

Time: 5 to 10 minutes

Materials: Disconnected telephone

Pick up a phone and say, "Just a minute. I'll see if he's home....There's a phone call for you, (your child's name)..." Continue the conversation until the child understands you are playing around and being silly and is enticed to join in.

Extensions:

- Let a favorite doll or stuffed animal have a turn on the phone.
- Make a call to a friend or family member and let the child hear the voice on the line.

Magic Bag

Time: 10 to 15 minutes

Materials: Old purse; small items that can't be swallowed, like model cars, playing cards, animal cookies, old key sets, little books

Your child will want to share the wonder of each discovery if you fill a purse with the small items (that are too big to be swallowed) and sit down to watch your child remove them and talk about each item that emerges.

Extensions:

- Stretch the vocabulary by using words like *inside, outside*, and *on top of* as you handle the items.
- Empty your pockets and talk about all the things you find there.
- Dress the child in clothing that has a pocket, and put something into it.
- Put the same item in both of your pockets and check back occasionally to see if you both still have them safe.

Silly Sounds

Time: 5 to 10 minutes

Materials: Books or magazines with pictures of familiar objects

While you are looking at pictures, imitate the sound of the objects you see and encourage your child to repeat them with you. For example, the dog goes, "woof-woof," and the car goes, "rrnnnn-rrnnnn."

Extensions:

- Ask your child how a car or dog sounds, helping out if needed.
- Get giggles by using nonsense words with regular inflections and a conversational tone.

Sniff and Tell

Time: 5 to 10 minutes

Materials: Several cotton balls, fragrances such as vanilla and lemon extract, cologne, vinegar, onion juice, lime juice

Young children can learn new words by experiencing smells. Sprinkle cotton balls with different scents and sit down together to take turns holding each ball under your noses and talking about your reactions.

Extensions:

- If there is another adult or child around, let your child share the cotton balls one at a time to see the reactions.
- Ask your child questions: "Which one do you like?" "Which one is yucky?"
- Encourage your child to smell food and talk about it.
- Offer a scented bubble bath or a dusting with bath powder.

Trying New Foods

Time: 15 to 30 minutes

Materials: Easily handled finger foods like slices of zucchini, apple slices with cinnamon, dabs of peanut butter, banana chunks, sliced lemons, pieces of cheese, etc.

Talk about the different tastes (sweet, hot, salty) and textures (crunchy, creamy, squishy) as you taste them together.

Extensions:

- Ask your child to tell you which ones are good and move them to one side.
- Have your child pick one that is left to give you a taste.
- Encourage your child to taste one of each.

Window of Opportunity

Time: 5 to 10 minutes

Materials: Window, comfortable chair

Go to a window together and look out while snuggling close. Talk about what you see together.

Extensions:

- If you don't mind the cleanup, put your mouths on the windows and breathe in and out, scribbling in the moisture that is left behind.
- Make a peek hole though the moisture for a tiny view of the world.
- Extend the child's vocabulary by using words to describe what you see: the fast, noisy, or big car, or the happy or angry child.
- Look for children who are passing by and point them out.

Coffee-Filter Painting

Time: 10 to 20 minutes

Materials: Paper coffee filters, at least 2 colors of water color or tempera paint ($), bulb basters or eye droppers

This kind of painting is magical, providing lots to talk about as the colors dance and blend. Put a small amount of paint in the baster or eyedropper and demonstrate how to drip it onto the filter. Repeat with another color. Fold over gently and pat, opening for a whole new design.

Extensions:

- Use colors like blue and yellow or red and blue that will blend into new colors.
- Talk about what the designs look like: butterflies, flowers, etc.
- Tape the dried filters to the windows so you can talk about how they look with the sun shining through them.
- Hang them about the house for decorations so that everyone can talk about them.

Flat Food

Time: 10 to 20 minutes

Materials: Old magazines with pictures to cut, paper plates, white glue

Search through magazines to find pictures of foods that the child likes to eat, cutting them out as you go. Pour a small amount of white glue on several paper plates and have your child spread it around with his fingers. Lay the pictures on the plates and let them dry. Have a party together and pretend to eat and enjoy the food.

Extensions:

- Invite dolls and stuffed animals to a party.
- Help your child sort the foods into breakfast, lunch, and dinner selections.
- Sort favorite foods into one pile and talk about them.
- Ask your child who would like to eat each food, thinking of other persons or pets.
- What would a princess like to eat? A giant? A mouse? Set a table for each.
- Play restaurant and let the child be the cook who delivers what you want.

Framed Foliage

Time: 1 hour

Materials: Leaves, wax paper ($), an iron, towel

This is a good activity for walking and talking together as you collect some seasonal leaves. Arrange the collected leaves attractively on a piece of wax paper. Cover with another piece of wax paper to form a sandwich. Fold a towel around the sandwich and move it to an ironing board. Iron the towel on medium heat until the wax paper underneath has fused together around the leaves.

Extensions:

- Add small torn pieces of colored gift or tissue paper.
- Frame and give as colorful gifts.
- Add a squirt of cologne or other scent before fusing and talk about the smell.
- Sprinkle with glitter ($) before heating.

Make a Face

Time: 5 to 10 minutes

Materials: None

Take turns making faces that express feelings like mad, happy, sad, or surprised.

Extensions:

- Find pictures of faces in a magazine that fit the words.
- Talk about how pets let us know how they are feeling.
- Talk about how babies communicate and how far your child has come in expressing needs and feelings.
- Talk about a particular incident and make the wrong face, asking the child for feedback. For instance, say that you fell down and hurt your knee and then smile.

Shrink and Grow

Time: 5 to 10 minutes

Materials: Simple drawings; computer, copy machine, or commercial copy center ($)

Use a copier or computer to enlarge drawings of small objects and shrink big ones. Talk about what the pictures look like before and after.

Extensions:

- Use a photograph of your child to shrink and enlarge. Talk about what you see.
- Challenge the child to curl into a ball and become small or stretch out as big as possible. Do this in front of a mirror.

Spicy

Time: 15 to 20 minutes

Materials: Any recipe that uses spices

Let your child help you to pour, stir, and add the spice to a recipe. Talk about the smells before and after the spice is added.

Extensions:

- Cook pancakes in several batches and add different spices to each, doing a taste test afterwards.
- Let your child use a pepper grinder to help you season a dish.
- Purchase fresh herbs in the store, and let the child smell and help add them to a recipe.

Things I Love

Time: 20 to 30 minutes

Materials: Collected leaves, feathers, or other outdoor items, needle and thread, a 2-yard piece of sheer fabric ($)

Make an unusual display of things your child has collected by sandwiching them between two layers of sheer fabric and sewing stitches to separate them from each other using little pockets. When hung on the wall, the display provides ongoing opportunities for the child to talk about the items.

Extension:

- Hang the display in front of a window so the light can shine through it.

You're the Star

Time: 5 to 10 minutes

Materials: None

Pick a favorite fairy tale and act out the story together, helping the child to talk about what the character feels.

Extension:

- Make up a story that you can act out for the child and talk about it together.

Basic Pretend Play

Time: 15 to 30 minutes

Materials: Props like scarves, hats, shoes, neckties, and shirts

Begin imaginary play with a simple offer like, "Let Mommy be the little girl and you be the mommy." Use symbolic props, like a block for a birthday cake, a stuffed animal for a pet, etc. Encourage suggestions by asking more questions. For instance, if your child invites you onto her bus, be sure to ask her where you are going to drive it and what you can do when you get there.

Extension:

- Add dolls or stuffed animals as characters with both of you making them talk.

Big Foot

Time: 15 to 20 minutes

Materials: Paper and pen

Help your child write down the shoe sizes of all family members. Talk about what is learned, explaining how adult and children's shoes are sized.

Extensions:

- Have your child collect a shoe from each person interviewed, and compare them by lining them up smallest to largest.
- Have family members line up bare-footed. Talk about the differences in feet.
- Paint the toenails for a festive look.
- Take turns giving foot massages with some nicely scented lotion.

Changing Shapes

Time: 5 to 10 minutes

Materials: 2 slices of bread, slices of individually wrapped cheese, butter or mustard, lettuce, plastic knife

Let your child cut the bread slices into triangles and the cheese to match it. Assemble sandwiches by adding butter or mustard and lettuce. Talk about how cutting made the shape change from a square to a triangle.

Extensions:

- Use a round cookie cutter or large glass to cut the bread and cheese into circles.
- Make a sandwich smaller by cutting it one more time. Are the new shapes the same as what you began with?
- Cut the sandwiches so that they are rectangles.

Dinnertime Talk

Time: 10 to 20 minutes

Materials: None

Dinnertime provides the perfect opportunity for your child to learn how to carry on conversations. Introduce an interesting topic, such as asking each person to share memories of their most memorable meal.

Extensions:

- Introduce other topics, like where each person would like to visit or who they would invite to dinner if they could.
- Take turns each night deciding on table topics.
- Write topics on slips of paper and take turns closing your eyes and selecting them.

Face File

Time: 15 to 30 minutes

Materials: Magazines that can be cut up, glue, thin cardboard

Cut out large pictures of eyes, noses, and mouths from the magazines. Paste together new faces and share what each one tells you.

Extensions:

- Store the faces in a folder and when your child is experiencing strong emotions, bring them out and match them to the child's mood, talking about what is felt.
- Talk about the different ways that people look, including hair, skin color, and size.

Fire Safety

Time: 15 to 20 minutes

Materials: Paper, a pencil or pen

Contact your local fire department, or check the Web for information about home fire safety. Talk about what you learn as it applies to your home.

Extensions:

- Practice a fire drill and discuss the results together.
- Help your child make a fire escape map of your home.
- Visit and make an escape map for a close family member in another home.

I Get Angry

Time: 10 to 20 minutes

Materials: None

Talk about hypothetical situations, determining which of them make each of you angry. Examples could include someone borrowing a favorite toy without asking, going to get ice cream in the refrigerator and finding it is all gone, raising a hand in class and not getting called on.

Extensions:

- Talk about the fact that everyone gets angry and share things that make you angry.
- Talk about acceptable and unacceptable reactions you have both seen.
- Challenge the child to come up with exciting, frustrating, and scary situations and acceptable responses.
- Find pictures in magazines to illustrate what you are talking about.
- Cut out pictures of an angry face and a happy face and take turns pointing to them in response to the situational questions.

It Felt Like...

Time: 10 to 20 minutes

Materials: Your child's favorite book

You can take a favorite story a step further after you read it by asking the child what a particular character felt like at some point in the story. Help to extend vocabulary as your child searches for ways to explain feelings.

Extensions:

- Make a list of words together that describe what a character felt.
- Ask the child if there is another way the story could have ended.
- Ask if there is another way a character could have acted.
- Ask the child how they feel about a particular part of a story.

Missing Words

Time: 5 to 10 minutes

Materials: None

Sing a familiar song or recite a poem and leave out a word. Challenge your child to fill in what is missing.

Extensions:

- Reverse roles and let your child challenge you with missing words.
- Insert a wrong word and challenge your child to identify it.
- Make up silly new words to insert together, letting your imaginations run wild.

One a Day

Time: A few minutes

Materials: None

Learning to communicate with new people can be difficult for young children. You can help by setting a goal of seeking out and talking together with your child to at least one new person a day. Over time, this could become a very useful habit.

Extensions:

- Help your child keep a list of who you talked to and where. At the end of the month, see if there are any patterns emerging.
- Talk about the quality of the conversation afterward. What felt good? Was anything left out? What would the child add, in hindsight?
- Visit a playground and encourage your child to talk to a child who is playing nearby. (This can be easier if the other child looks younger, and you can suggest something specific to say such as, "Hello, my name is....")
- At a playground, sit near another child and begin to talk so your child can come over and join in.

Personal Placemats

Time: 30 minutes

Materials: Sturdy piece of cardboard the size of a placemat (white gift boxes work well for this), photographs, felt pens ($), clear plastic contact paper ($)

Create personal placemats while learning things about each other as you go. Arrange photos, magazine pictures, cartoons, and stickers on the cardboard and decorate with felt pens. Seal both sides into a piece of contact paper about 1 inch larger than the mat. Fold the extra contact paper to the back.

Extensions:

- These make nice gifts. Talk to your child about someone you could make one for and about what sorts of things should be included.
- Add the child's name and hang it on the bedroom door to identify their space.
- Stars ($), stickers ($) or glitter ($) add a festive touch.

Seed Hunt

Time: 30 minutes to 1 hour

Material: Bag for collecting, white glue, paper, wax paper ($)

Take a nature walk together to look for seeds and glue them onto sheets of wax paper for displaying.

Extensions:

- Use art paper and white glue to make collages of the seeds you bring back. Talk to the child about what each of you is doing as you build the collages.
- Check out a library book before you go out to walk.
- Glue seeds together on pieces of wax paper and let dry. Remove and insert a hook to hang for decorations.
- Glue seeds in a line on a piece of paper from smallest to largest.

Sizzler

Time: 10 to 15 minutes

Materials: Baking soda, vinegar, eyedropper

This exciting experiment can make the words flow as quickly as the bubbles. Have your child put a small amount of baking soda in a bowl and drop on a few drops of vinegar with the dropper. Fizzles will follow from the chemical reaction.

Extensions:

- Add a drop or 2 of food coloring to the vinegar.
- Think of words to talk about what is happening. Introduce words like sizzle and foam that the child may not know.

Switch Roles

Time: 10 minutes

Materials: None

When you and your child disagree, suggest that you switch roles for a few minutes and help your child rethink what is going on by prompting new responses.

Extension:

- When your child has some practice doing this, agree that either of you can call a *Switch Roles* when needed.

Trail Mix

Time: 15 to 30 minutes

Materials: Variety of healthy ingredients ($) such as diced dried fruit, nonsugar cereal, nuts or seeds, plastic measuring cup, large bowl, snack-sized baggies

This activity can be used to bring out language about the feel of the ingredients, about nutrition, and about words used in cooking tasks like measuring and mixing. Wash hands and then guide the child in using a measuring cup to assemble 3 parts cereal, 1 part dried fruit and 1 part nuts or seeds into a large bowl. Mix with the hands and scoop and seal into plastic bags.

Extensions:

- For a sweeter mix as a special treat, add 1 part small carob or butterscotch chips or grated coconut.
- Talk about the tastes of the different ingredients. Use words to describe the tastes, like salty, chewy, and hard.
- Help your child to draw a picture of this recipe for future use, with illustrations of measuring cups and ingredients.
- Make a list of people to deliver bags of the snack to and cross off each name as you go.

What I Want

Time: A few minutes

Materials: None

Learning to ask others for what you need comes from practice. Talk to the child about what they would like to order when you take them to a restaurant and give them a turn at ordering for themselves.

Extensions:

- Ask the child to order a single item for you.
- Let the child choose one thing to purchase when visiting a store and talk to you about why it was chosen.
- Plan a birthday party or other outing together, helping the child to list all the things that could be included to make it a successful party.

kindergarten through grade 3

Earth Bowl

Time: Several hours

Materials: 4-ounce packages of raspberry and lemon gelatin dessert mix ($), 8-ounce package black cherry gelatin dessert mix ($), 4 cups of boiling water, 4 cups of cold water, 3 mixing bowls, 12 graham crackers ($), ½ cup melted butter, ¼ cup sugar, a 10-inch-diameter glass bowl

This activity lets you talk about geology and natural science in a fun way. Prepare the gelatin desserts in separate bowls according to box directions. Put into the refrigerator to set. Crush the graham crackers into fine crumbs and mix with the melted butter and sugar. Press into the bottom and along the sides of the glass bowl. Set aside. In about 2 hours, spoon the black cherry gelatin into the crust, leaving a 5-inch pocket in the middle. Spoon in the lemon gelatin, leaving a 2-inch hole. Spoon the raspberry gelatin into the hole. Allow to set before dipping briefly into warm water to loosen and unmold by inverting.

The graham cracker crust represents the crust, which is about 20 miles deep. The black cherry is the mantle, which is 4,000 miles deep. The lemon is the outer core, which is about 2,000 miles deep, and the raspberry is the inner core, which is about 800 miles deep.

Extension:

- Share the dessert with someone and help your child (if needed) to tell the person about the earth's geological layers.

Family Hand Prints

Time: 15 to 20 minutes

Materials: Felt pen ($), paper

This activity is always a hit, but when you include family members, the learning is extended automatically. Help your child trace around one hand with the felt pen. Do the same for the other family members and talk about the results.

Extensions:

- Help your child draw around a favorite toy, doll, or stuffed animal. Was it difficult or easy to do?
- Help your child trace around a fruit or vegetable and talk about what it looks like. Cut the fruit or vegetable in half and talk about why that makes it easier.
- Go outside together and find things to collect and trace around.

First to See

Time: 10 to 15 minutes

Materials: None

This is a fun game to play in the car or while taking a walk. Think of an object, and the first one to see it gets to pick the next object to search for.

Extensions:

- Change the rule to be the first one who sees an object 3 times.
- Make it the first one to see 3 items in a sequence, like a car, baby, and an airplane.

I Could Have...

Time: 5 to 15 minutes

Materials: None

To encourage good problem solving, you can help your child learn the value of asking questions and discussing information involved in a situation. Sit down with your child when a poor choice has been made and discuss other choices that could have been made. Children feel valued when adults take the time to help them process through issues, especially when the adults respect the answers that the children come up with.

Extensions:

- Write down what your child says and save it in a box or binder to refer to later when a similar choice comes up.
- Take turns making up hypothetical situations for each of you to respond to.

Introducing

Time: 10 to 15 minutes

Materials: None

Take turns introducing each other while pretending you are on a stage. Stand up, bow, and tell all the good things you can about the other person, his hobbies, good qualities, etc. Be sure to over-dramatize.

Extensions:

- Take turns introducing other family members, present or not.
- Challenge your child to introduce a best friend or a favorite teacher.
- Think of famous people and take turns introducing them.

Job Search

Time: 15 to 20 minutes

Materials: Classified employment ads from a newspaper

Spread out the employment ads and search for 3 jobs that your child thinks would be fun. Talk about what each of you thinks that the job entails and why it would be fun.

Extensions:

- Do a mock interview with your child as the job applicant.
- Talk about work hours, salary, and benefits that should go with the job.
- Share what each of you thinks would be the best job in the world and why.
- Talk about the jobs that you and other family members have now or have had in the past.
- Ask your child about future career choices and wishes.

Kitchen-Talk

Time: Varies

Materials: Whatever you are planning to cook

You can expose your child to cooking words by allowing them to perform the actions that accompany them. Talk about and perform actions like mixing, chopping, peeling, stirring, washing, tossing, whipping, draining, shaking, mashing, straining, turning, measuring, kneading, unscrewing, leveling, squeezing, pouring, packing, rolling, dipping, cutting, grating, scrubbing, slicing, cracking, tearing, breaking, snapping, or wrapping.

Extensions:

- Give your child a kitchen tool and talk about what it does, using as many new cooking words as possible.
- Watch a chef on television and talk about similarities and differences in the cooking show and your kitchen routines.

Mystery Messages

Time: 5 to 10 minutes

Materials: Paper, pencil, tape, breakfast food

Surprise the child with a mystery hunt that begins upon rising in the morning and ends with a special breakfast. The first direction should be visible near the bed or bathroom and the game should continue with additional message clues throughout the house. This is an excellent way to begin celebrating your child's birthday.

Extensions:

- Use this technique for giving surprises or gifts.
- Adapt the game for an easy bedtime routine that goes to the pajama drawer, toothbrush, and ends with a storybook

Personal Calendar

Time: 1 hour

Materials: White paper, ruler, adhesive tape or glue, favorite photograph, pencil, small piece of string

Good communication skills are built during the process of planning ahead for an activity. Allow your child to select a favorite photograph for the top of a calendar and work together drawing a calendar grid with 7 squares across and five down. Fill in the name of the month, the days of the week, and the numbers.

Your child can draw decorations around the photograph and draw symbols or pictures to denote weekend (nonschool) days, special holidays, birthdays, etc. Talk about what your child thinks is important enough to be put on the calendar and provide examples if help is needed.

Extensions:

- Tie the pencil through a hole punched in the bottom of the page so your child can "X" through each square at the end of the day, talking about things that have happened.
- Ask your child questions about the upcoming week, counting the days until anticipated events will happen.
- Add bedtimes to reflect differences on weekends and holidays.

Picture the Action

Time: 15 to 30 minutes

Materials: None

Storytelling frees your child's imagination from someone else's concepts. Begin a story anywhere. You don't need to know where you are going as the child will be happy to help you move the story along. A good way to get started is to talk about things you did when you were a child.

Extensions:

- Draw pictures of the story when you are finished and share them with each other.
- Talk about similarities and differences in your 2 different stories.
- Make up stories about what might be possible far off into your futures.

Picture Walks

Time: 30 minutes to 1 hour

Materials: Paper; writing or drawing utensils

Take a walk together and when you are finished, sit down and draw pictures of what you saw, being careful not to look at each other's drawings until you are finished. Talk about the different ways that people see the same things.

Extensions:

- Pick one thing that you both noticed on the walk and draw how it looked to each of you, sharing what was the same and what was different.
- Share a picture of the most beautiful thing you saw, the most interesting, the most exciting, etc.

Quilt of Many Feelings

Time: 20 to 30 minutes

Materials: Colored paper ($), felt pens ($), white glue

Traditionally, making quilts has been a way for people to express themselves through the use of color and pattern. A quilt of faces can help your child understand how emotions are conveyed through facial expressions. Give the child pieces of light-colored paper cut into 6-inch squares. Draw faces on each piece of paper to resemble feelings each of you sometimes feel and arrange them on a large piece of paper so that they resemble a patchwork quilt. Hang the quilt in a conspicuous place where it can be a source of future conversations.

Extensions:

- Make a feelings quilt for someone else and decide together what it should be like so it reflects them. Deliver it together.
- Make a feelings quilt for a holiday decoration, using the symbols and cultural items associated with it.

Secret Society

Time: 15 to 30 minutes

Materials: Writing materials

During the early school-age years, children love secret clubs. Form one together and make up a password, code, handshake, or other secrets.

Extension:

- Help your child think of a secret club that could be shared with a few friends and help just enough to get them started.
- Designate a secret meeting place for the club that is as private and interesting as possible.

Shop and Feel

Time: 30 minutes

Materials: None

As you buy items at the grocery store, let your child handle them. Ask what each item feels like, suggesting words when vocabulary is needed. Suggestions could include cold milk, the rough skin of a cantaloupe, and a light bag of chips.

Extensions:

- Have your child feel items with his eyes closed and describe them.
- Have your child sniff with his eyes closed to see if the food can be identified.
- Let your child feel several of the same item, such as potatoes or melons, and tell you which one to buy and why.
- Ask your child to look in the shopping basket and guess which item is likely to be the heaviest or the lightest. Check it out on the produce scale.

Sound Bytes

Time: 30 minutes

Materials: Small tape recorder ($)

Give your child a recorder with a few tapes and demonstrate how to tape voices during family interviews.

Extensions:

- Talk about the interviews after listening to them. Find similarities and differences in the responses.
- Challenge your child to record sounds around the house (a flushing toilet, the garbage disposal, peeling a carrot, etc.).
- Use the final tape to play a guessing game.
- Take turns recording voices and guessing whom they belong to.

Talk It Out

Time: 15 to 30 minutes

Materials: Favorite stuffed animal or doll

You can use a favorite stuffed animal to help your child express things that are difficult to talk about. Many children will open up more easily with this simple way to buffer personal feelings.

Extensions:

- Use two stuffed animals and let them talk to each other about an issue.
- Designate dolls with a particular function, like the silly doll or the serious doll.
- A puppet can make a good "mediator" in difficult situations.

Time Capsule

Time: 30 minutes to an hour

Materials: A few of your child's favorite things

Make a time capsule together and be sure to include a few of your child's favorite things. Help your child to write a letter describing her favorite activities, friends, subjects, teacher, etc. Date the capsule, seal it with heavy tape, and put it away for a year, labeling it with the date you will open it. This activity guarantees that you will be talking during and afterward.

Extensions:

- Have your child help to make a time capsule for you, selecting things that you care about.
- Talk about what you would both put into a capsule for your neighborhood, city, or country.
- Discuss what an imaginary character on television or in a book would put into a time capsule.

WEIGHTY MATTERS

Time: 30 minutes

Materials: Small scale ($), objects to weigh, paper, pencil or pen

Show the child how to use and balance the scale carefully, stressing its delicacy. Besides learning a bit of physics, this activity encourages your child to describe new concepts. Let your child weigh the objects and chart the results on paper.

Extensions:

- Challenge your child to gather additional items to weigh and chart.
- See which of you can find the lightest thing that fills up a hand or the heaviest that fits into a small box. Check it out to be sure.
- Have your child weigh in on the family scale and compare that weight to his birth weight and other records you may have of his weight as he grew.

6 concentration

Concentration is rarely natural for young children, and cultivating it will always present you with challenges. Nevertheless, it is worthwhile, since the ability to focus and complete a task is critical, particularly in early school experiences. Being with children requires a great deal of stamina and creativity because they crave novelty and stimulation and are easily bored. Their play often looks somewhat haphazard as they bounce from activity to activity with irritation and whining in between.

The concept of *attention span* was proposed as early as 1894 by developmentalist James Mark Baldwin when he noted differences in the extent to which children remain engaged in activities and returned to them after interruption. That means that blaming television and electronic gadgets for hyperactivity may not get to the root cause, the natural restlessness of the young child at play.

The road to learning concentration is a long one, but the journey can be started in the earliest years, although personality can limit your success from stage to stage. Highly active children present formidable challenges in this area. But don't despair. This chapter offers play activities that have clear beginnings, middles, and endings, allowing children to experience activity completion and the satisfaction that it brings.

As focus and completion are experienced again and again, the satisfaction that follows is anticipated and enjoyed.

The activities in this chapter require your active participation and continual encouragement, perhaps more so than with any of the other six skills. It is important for you to be fully present so you can monitor the pace and celebrate the victories. The payoff is well worth your time, for children who learn to focus and complete tasks do better in school and are better equipped to control impulses and to delay gratification throughout their lives.

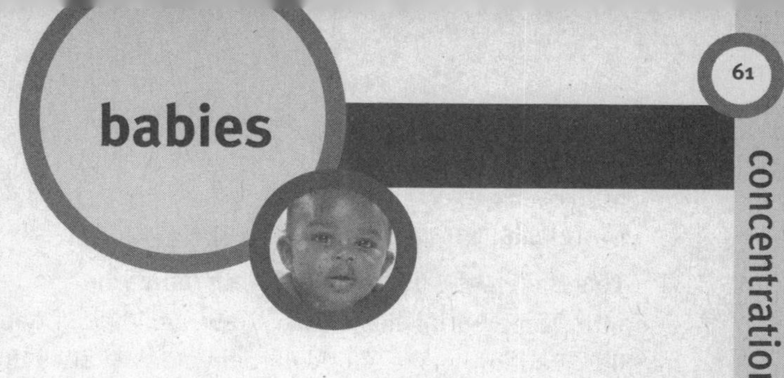

Brush Our Teeth

Time: 5 to 10 minutes

Materials: 2 toothbrushes, toothpaste

With the appearance of the first tooth comes the need to begin brushing it. One way to help a child concentrate on the task is to do it together in front of a mirror.

Extensions:

- Brush each other's teeth, keeping toothbrushes separate to model good hygiene.
- Brush the teeth on a doll or stuffed animal, talking about what you are doing.

Busy Fingers

Time: 5 to 10 minutes

Materials: Handful of unsweetened cereal pieces

This is an old stand-by but one that requires intense concentration with a built-in reward. It helps the baby to develop hand-eye coordination that is needed in so many upcoming tasks. Spread some cereal out on the high chair tray or other play area and let the baby pick up the pieces and pop them into her mouth.

Extensions:

- Put a few pieces of cereal in a container like a small box or open pouch so that the baby can dig inside for the treats.
- Put some pieces into a closed plastic container and shake it before opening it to show the baby what is inside. As the baby eats, close and repeat now and then.
- Ask the baby to put one in your mouth, and help, if necessary.
- Lay out 2 or 3 cups and show the baby how to put cereal pieces into each one.

Fast-Food Fun

Time: 5 to 10 minutes

Materials: Straw, 3 or 4 plastic lid tops

This is a great way to distract your baby when you are out to eat at a fast food restaurant. Thread drink lids onto a straw and let your baby play with it and try to remove the lids. Caution: make sure your baby doesn't stick the straws down her throat.

Extensions:

- Replace the straws when they are all removed and begin again.
- Put several assembled lids and straws in front of your baby.

First Hide and Seek

Time: 5 to 10 minutes

Materials: Common household objects

This seems simple, but when you see how much your baby focuses on this game, you will love to play it, too. Place a bright-colored object in one of your pockets, making sure that part of it is showing. Ask the baby where it is, and when you pull it out of its hiding place, show your excitement. Repeat.

Extensions:

- Hide it again, letting the baby see you do it and ask the baby to find the toy, showing great excitement when it is found.
- Hide the toy in a different spot, making sure it is still slightly visible.
- Put the object under your shirt.

First Hole and Peg

Time: 5 to 10 minutes

Materials: 3 empty toilet-paper rolls, a shoe box

In the top of the box cut 3 holes that are big enough for an empty toilet-paper roll to slide through easily. Sit on the floor together and show the child how to put a roll into each hole.

Extensions:

- Shake the box, open it, and let your child pull the rolls out and repeat.
- Take turns putting the rolls into the box, talking about who is doing it each time.

Footsies

Time: 5 to 10 minutes

Materials: Brightly colored baby sock or bootie

When your baby is lying on his back, put a brightly colored sock or bootie on one foot and lightly grasp the toes of the foot to draw attention to the bootie. Join in the fun once it is noticed. Ask, "What have you got there?"

Extensions:

- Tap the toes of the 2 feet together.
- Hold the foot and tickle the toes by gently nuzzling them.
- Add a second bright sock of a different color on the other foot.

Look Away

Time: 5 minutes

Materials: None

Even very young babies will look away and break eye contact when over-stimulated. When your baby looks away, say, "Okay, (your child's name) is done playing now." Follow with a nice hug.

Extensions:

- If the attention returns, acknowledge your excitement and appreciation.
- Reward your baby's communication by offering something comforting, like a blanket or bottle.

Restaurant Essentials

Time: 5 to 10 minutes

Materials: Baby's spoon, bib, rattles

Eating out with baby will be easier if you bring along a few familiar mealtime helpers so the baby is not so distracted and stimulated by all that is going on and has a frame of reference about what is expected.

Spaghetti Pick-Up

Time: 5 to 10 minutes

Materials: Pieces of cooked spaghetti (for babies who are able to eat finger foods)

Many babies will stick to this activity until they succeed. Place a few strands of the cooked spaghetti in front of the baby at the highchair or table. Let the baby experiment with picking up the pieces and eating them. If necessary, cut the pieces into sizes that can be easily swallowed.

Extensions:

- Cover the spaghetti with an inverted plastic bowl and let the child discover it.
- Pull your baby's two hands gently together and place a fistful of the spaghetti in them.
- Cut one piece of spaghetti into smaller pieces.
- Say, "Give me one," and slurp it up when it is put into your mouth.

Ticking Away

Time: 5 minutes

Materials: Ticking clock

Hide a fairly loud ticking clock behind your back and ask your baby what the sound is, bringing it out to show the source of the sound.

Extensions:

- Hide the clock under a blanket and let your baby find it.
- Hide it in a shoe box nearby and encourage exploration by asking about the sound.
- Put it under your shirt and let your baby find it.

Buy Some Time

Time: 5 to 10 minutes

Materials: Jar of bubble mix with wand ($), masking tape, newspaper, hand-sized household items

When you need just a few moments to finish a task or phone conversation, place your toddler near to you and blow a few bubbles, or pass single pieces of newspaper to crumple and short strips of masking tape to stick about.

Clothespin Drop

Time: 10 to 15 minutes

Materials: Large coffee can, nonspring clothespins

This seemingly simple task helps with hand-eye coordination. Put clothespins around the neck of a large coffee can and show the toddler how to take them off, one at a time, and drop them into the can.

Extensions:

- Dump out the clothespins and replace them so the game can continue.
- Challenge the child to replace the pins on the can's edge.
- Drop the pins, one at a time, into the can from a standing position.
- Drop the pins from a sitting position.

Cross the River

Time: 5 to 10 minutes

Materials: Thin cardboard or heavy paper, scissors, masking tape

Cut out several 8- to 10-inch circles and tape them to the floor in a straight line so that they are close enough to move from one to the other in a step. Pretend they are stepping stones across a river and take turns crossing over the whole line of them.

Extensions:

- Place the circles into a gentle curve and step from one to another.
- If your toddler is able, have her alternate steps, putting only one foot on a dot.
- Play stop and go as your toddler moves about on the dots.
- Tell your toddler to lead so that you can follow.
- Move across the circles using music of different tempos.

Moving So Carefully

Time: 5 to 10 minutes

Materials: Cup, water, masking tape

Tape a finish line to the floor or sidewalk and give your toddler a cup that is nearly full of water. The challenge is to walk to the line, spilling as little as possible.

Extensions:

- Increase the challenge by holding a cup of water in each hand.
- Walk around an obstacle with the cup of water.
- Compare by carrying an empty cup and talk about the difference.
- Walk together holding cups of water.

Rise and Fall

Time: 5 minutes

Materials: Small hand drum ($) or other object to beat

Lie down together on your stomachs and beat the drum twice. On the first beat, raise the stomach off the floor. On the second beat, bring it back down flat. Let your toddler feel your tummy go up and down with the count.

Extensions:

- Repeat, lying on your backs with shirts pulled up to expose the stomach.
- Decide on another body part to raise and lower on the two beats.
- One of you be the leader, with the other copying the movements.
- Put a small toy on the tummy and see if you can keep it from falling off.

Seesaw

Time: 5 minutes

Materials: None

Sit on the floor facing each other and hold hands. Lean forward so your toddler goes back and reverse the process in a seesaw motion.

Extensions:

- Take turns taking the lead and deciding how fast to go.
- Use a scarf to hold onto while rocking back and forth.
- Sing a simple song to the beat of your movements.

Soapy Songs

Time: 10 to 15 minutes

Materials: Bathtub

During bath time and to the tune of, "Here We Go 'round the Mulberry Bush," sing, "This is the way we wash our toes..."

Extensions:

- Repeat the song with different body parts (tummy, feet, arms, etc.) and follow each chorus by asking your toddler where a particular body part is.
- Repeat the game when drying with a towel, adapting the words.

Spoons Away

Time: 5 to 10 minutes

Materials: Large spoon, large bowl, wide-mouthed cup

You may want to do this one outside, at a table, or on the lawn. Place a bowl of water in front of your toddler with the spoon. Demonstrate how to use the spoon to transfer the water out of the bowl and into the cup.

Extensions:

- Add some ice cubes.
- Add food coloring.
- Add scented cooking extract.
- Change the size of the spoon.
- Offer a soup ladle.

Tunnel Fun

Time: 5 to 10 minutes

Materials: Large packing box, familiar household object or toy

This activity promotes mindful control of the body in a limited space. Cut off the ends of a large cardboard box and set it down so it makes a tunnel. Put one of your toddler's favorite toys at one end of the box and encourage crawling through to get it. Be sure to check for and remove any protruding staples before you begin.

Extensions:

- Gently and slowly roll the box over with your toddler inside, talking about what you are doing and saying, "Here we go."
- Challenge your toddler to crawl in backward. You may have to show them how.
- Invite your toddler to bring a stuffed-animal friend and a comfortable blanket into the box.

Waiting for Food

Time: 5 to 10 minutes

Materials: Paper napkin

While waiting for food to arrive, open up a paper napkin and fold it as many times as you can, looking at the design after it is reopened.

Extensions:

- Fold back and forth to make a fan.
- Squeeze it hard in your hands to make it as small as you can and then release it.

Walk the Plank

Time: 10 to 15 minutes

Materials: Flat piece of wood that is at least an inch thick and 5 feet long

Lay the board on the grass or indoors on a rug and show your toddler how to walk across it with your hands extended to the sides for balance.

Extensions:

- Use towels to raise the plank an inch or two.
- Show how to walk the plank with 1 foot on and 1 foot off.
- Try holding hands while you both walk across sideways.
- Walk the plank barefoot.

Boredom Buster

Time: 15 to 30 minutes

Materials: Shoe box with little toys, cookies, etc.

Keep this surprise box off-limits until it is needed so that the contents remain new and interesting. Rotate and change the contents from time to time.

Extension:

- Keep boredom boxes in the car, by the phone, or near your shower.
- Color the box to personalize it for your child.

Bull's-Eye

Time: 15 to 20 minutes

Materials: Variety of hand-sized sponges, bucket of water, chalk ($)

Draw a target on outdoor pavement. Soak the sponges in the bucket of water and toss them into the center of the target.

Extensions:

- Play until the bull's-eye is erased.
- Draw the target on a wall for a different throwing experience.
- Alternate turns for 2 throws, letting the child keep track of who is up next.

Card Drop

Time: 10 to 15 minutes

Materials: Deck of playing cards, shoe box, scissors

Handling each card separately will be a big challenge. Cut a fairly large slit in the top of a shoe box and show your toddler how to drop playing cards through the hole.

Extensions:

- When you have finished, shake the box, asking your child what is inside. Let the child open the lid to find the cards and repeat the game.
- Have your child find as many "picture" cards as possible and put only them in the box.
- Take turns putting cards in the box.

Careful Walking

Time: 5 to 10 minutes

Materials: Chalk ($) or masking tape

Make a line and take turns walking on it with the toes pointed outward.

Extensions:

- Walk with the toes pointed in.
- Walk with the toes straight ahead.
- Walk with the toes curled under.
- Walk with the feet crossing over the line, left over right and then right over left.

Color Walk

Time: 10 to 20 minutes

Materials: Small, solid-colored piece of cloth

Pin or tie the colored cloth to the sleeve and talk about the color of the cloth as you look around the house for items of the same color.

Extensions:

- Make a list of the things that you found and review it when you are finished.
- Go around the house with a basket and find things of that color to put into it.
- Do a color hunt in the child's room.
- Have your child pick a favorite piece of clothing to match items to.

Crawling Under

Time: 10 to 15 minutes

Materials: Table

A low table can provide a good tool for letting the child discover information about moving deliberately and with concentration. Simply have your toddler crawl under the table from one end to the other. There is no single right way to do this and creativity will emerge with experimentation.

Extension:

- Use a sawhorse, card table, or any combination of low objects to do the activity.

Dinnertime Stroll

Time: 10 to 15 minutes

Materials: Dinner out at a restaurant

When going to a restaurant, it will help if a family member takes the child for a walk outside after the food has been ordered. When the food arrives, your child will have an easier time sitting still and focusing on eating.

Easy Rhythm Instruments

Time: 5 to 10 minutes

Materials: Objects to hit together such as small pots and pans, aluminum tins, spoon and a small box, metal salt shaker filled with rice, two wooden spoons

Young children have natural rhythm, and if you put on some music and offer these "instruments," you can have fun moving playfully together.

Extensions:

- Trade instruments or exchange them for others.
- Take them outside and march barefoot across the grass.

Empty and Full

Time: 10 to 15 minutes

Materials: Cotton balls, plastic sandwich bags

Work together to fill the sandwich bags with cotton balls, one at a time. It is surprising how long this seemingly simple activity can take and how focused your child can become.

Extensions:

- Ask your child to find something else to put the cotton balls into.
- Give your child a sock to fill with cotton balls.
- If either of you have pockets, fill them with cotton balls.
- Let your child fill a purse or pocketbook when you have to wait for an appointment.

Exploring Space

Time: 5 to 15 minutes

Materials: One or more old automobile tires

Control of the arms and legs at the same time presents many challenges to the toddler, who loves to climb in and out of things. Lay the tire(s) flat on the ground and encourage your child to explore by climbing in, on, and out.

Extensions:

- Encourage your child to jump from the edge.
- Have your child sit in the middle and wave to you.
- Join in the fun so the child can observe your body at work.
- Lie down next to each other on some tires and look straight up to the sky, talking about what you see.
- Turn over and share what you see on the ground, up close.

First Basketball Drop

Time: 5 to 10 minutes

Materials: Wastebasket or cardboard box, small softball

The refinement of ball skills is still years away, but it's not too early to foster a familiarity with the control needed for ball play. Offer the child several balls to throw or drop into the container. Dump them out and repeat again.

Extensions:

- Use balls of different sizes.
- Roll the ball(s) toward the container and then drop them in.
- Hold your child (balanced on a chair, if necessary) over the container and let her drop the balls into it.
- Use small balls and a bucket to play the game in the bathtub.

Homemade Finger Paint

Time: 30 minutes to 1 hour or more

Materials: ½ cup of cornstarch, very cold water, small jars for each color, food coloring ($) or powdered tempera paint ($), finger-paint paper ($) (available at art or toy stores)

Finger painting is calming and promotes a high level of concentration. You will need to either supervise or do the cooking. Mix the cornstarch with 4 cups of ice cold water. Put into a pot and turn the heat on high. Bring to a boil and stir until it thickens. Allow the mixture to cool and pour some into each jar. Add several drops of food coloring or a little tempera paint to each jar and mix. Makes enough paint for about 6 colors.

Extensions:

- Pour a small amount of the uncolored paint onto the paper and sprinkle with powdered tempera paint or drops of food coloring. Let your child mix the color with his fingers.
- Add additional colors one at a time so your child can discover the new colors that emerge.

I Can Pour

Time: 15 to 20 minutes

Materials: Large plastic bowls, assorted plastic containers with wide mouths, 1- and 2-cup plastic measuring cups, water

Pouring is a highly creative exercise for toddlers who are not yet familiar with what is involved in the transfer of materials. It is a skill that is learned with a great deal of practice over time. Have your toddler pour different amounts of water from one container to another.

Extensions:

- Use rice or beans to experience more control.
- Graduate to pouring sand.
- Offer additional tools, cups, ladles, etc.
- Use dry cereal, raisins, or miniature marshmallows that can be eaten during the play.

Inside-Out

Time: 10 to 15 minutes

Materials: None

Take a walk to the back of the house and ask your child to guess which room is behind each window.

Extensions:

- If possible, lift your child so the guess can be confirmed.
- Hang pictures on a window and go outside to see them.

In the Slot

Time: 10 to 15 minutes

Materials: Poker chips, empty coffee can with plastic lid, scissors or knife

This activity challenges emerging fine motor skills and requires that your child sit still and work patiently. Cut a 2 by ¼–inch slot in the plastic lid and put it back on the container. Show your child that the plastic poker chips can be dropped through the slot in the container.

Extensions:

- When all the chips are inside, help your child take off the lid, dump them out, and begin again.
- Ask your child to shake the can as hard as he can, making a "big" noise.
- Have your child arrange the poker chips around the base of the can in a circle.

Jump Off

Time: 5 to 10 minutes

Materials: Low surface (about 6 to 8 inches high) to jump off

Jumping is a beloved skill that you might as well encourage in a controlled environment, as they are going to try it anyway. Have your child move about the surface to get comfortable. Offer a hand during the first few tries.

Extensions:

- Help your child to jump forward onto a pillow.
- Encourage a jump into your arms from a chair.
- Share your child's hands with another adult and help to jump high.

Just So

Time: 10 to 15 minutes

Materials: Plastic tub or sink with water, indelible marker, several plastic cups

Draw a fill line on several of the cups and let your child use the remaining cups to pour water just to the lines.

Extensions:

- Count out loud how many cups are full to their lines with the toddler.
- Add food coloring so it is easier to see the water level.

MAGIC TUBE

Time: 10 to 15 minutes

Materials: Long mailing tube with the plastic ends removed, a few small plastic or metal cars ($)

Not only does this game challenge concentration and motor coordination, but it also holds a surprise reward when the car zips out the other end. Hold the tube slightly elevated on one side and pass small metal cars through it, one at a time. Your child will love watching the cars go in one side and come out the other.

Extensions:

- You hold the tube and let your child put the cars in.
- Count the cars out loud as you put them in.
- Cover both ends and shake the tube, asking your child where the cars are.
- Put a bucket or box at the end of the tube so the cars roll into it.
- Brace the tube against a chair so the cars can fly out the end.

MATCHING SOCKS

Time: 10 minutes

Materials: 5 pairs of distinctively different socks

This is a good way to play for a few minutes while you are folding the laundry. Put the socks in front of your child and work together to find the matching pairs.

Extensions:

- Use socks that are still warm out of the dryer.
- Roll each pair into a ball and bat it back and forth.
- Encourage your child to take the balls apart.
- Put them back together and let your child put them into the drawers where they belong.
- Compare the sock size of each family member by lining them up and talking about what you see.
- Have your child sort the matched pairs according to color.
- Use large clothespins to clip the pairs together

My Number Book

Time: 15 to 20 minutes

Materials: Magazines or newspapers, scissors, paper, glue

Search through magazines and newspapers and find the numerals 1 through 10. Cut out each number and glue all of them onto separate sheets of paper.

Extensions:

- Go back and find pictures for each number and glue them on the corresponding pages. For example, two flowers, four mouths.
- Mix them up and see if you can put them in order again.

Number Salad

Time: 20 to 30 minutes

Materials: Orange, apple, banana, grapes, grated coconut, cheese, miniature marshmallows, orange juice

This recipe reinforces the concept of each numeral from 1 through 10. Have the child mix the following quantities into a bowl: 1 handful toasted coconut, 2 tablespoons orange juice, 3 orange sections, 4 apple slices, 5 cheese cubes, 6 banana slices, 7 miniature marshmallows, 8 seedless grapes, stir 9 times, and (10) eat!

Extensions:

- Help your child to pick a number and some ingredients for a snack and work out a recipe of his own, as above.
- Make up your own number recipes by setting out foods that your child can choose from.

Rice Games

Time: 20 to 30 minutes

Materials: Large bowl, raw rice, funnel, 8 to 10 small jars, rubber bands

Set out a large bowl about ⅓ full of rice. Use rubber bands to make measuring lines on the jars and fill the jars up to those lines using the funnel.

Extensions:

- Ask follow-up questions: Which jar has the most? Which has the least? Are there any that have the same amount? Which jar was filled first? Which last?
- Experiment with ways to fill up the jars without the funnel. Talk about the results.

Soft Floating Bubbles

Time: 10 to 20 minutes

Materials: Jar of bubbles that includes a wand ($)

Floating is a concept that captures the imagination of even the youngest of children. Blow bubbles so your toddler can watch them move in slow motion through the air.

Extensions:

- Put on some soft and soothing music and move like the bubbles.
- Turn a fan on low and let it do the work for you.

Stacking Boxes

Time: 10 to 20 minutes

Materials: 6 medium-sized empty boxes or food containers

This is block building of a different sort, and it takes a great deal of self-control to accomplish the task. Close the lids on each box and set them out, showing your child how to stack them one on top of the other until they fall down—which is also part of the fun.

Extensions:

- Take turns putting a box on the pile.
- Make a train and push it from the rear "car."
- Pretend you are giving presents to each other. You can pretend by putting a toy or other household object in the box.

Taking Turns

Time: 10 to 15 minutes

Materials: Hat

Use the hat to signify that you are the leader so your child can copy your movements.

Extensions:

- Let your child take a turn wearing the hat and being the leader.
- Add a third person to make the sharing 3-way.
- Use the leader's hat at the dinner table to take turns talking.

Tense and Release

Time: 10 to 15 minutes

Materials: None

You can help children experience the physical changes that happen when their bodies are tense and relaxed. Lie down together on your backs and make a face holding it and then releasing quickly on command. Tighten the fingers and arms and relax in the same way, on command. Do the same thing with the legs and feet. Finally, breathe in deeply and tighten the whole body from head to toe and hold. Relax and force all of the air out of the lungs. Talk to the child about what it felt like.

Extensions:

- Let your child stand and feel your legs tensed and relaxed.
- Repeat from a standing position

Triangle Hunt

Time: 15 to 30 minutes

Materials: Picture of a triangle-shaped object

Show your child the shape of a triangle and trace it together with your fingers. Using the picture as a model, hunt for similar shapes in the room.

Extensions:

- The same activity can be done by taking a walk at the mall or around the neighborhood.
- Work your way through your child's toy box searching for a shape.
- Search through the refrigerator.

Up and Down

Time: 15 to 20 minutes

Materials: Low stepladder, footstool, chair, or table

This activity should be done on a soft surface, as falls are part of the experience. Offer a hand, if needed, and encourage your child to climb and descend from the surface.

Extensions:

- Use a favorite stuffed animal to join in the fun.
- Count the steps as your child moves up and down.
- Try alternating steps with putting both feet on a single step.

Wash the Clothes

Time: 20 minutes

Materials: Plastic tub or wash basin, detergent, few small pieces of laundry such as dishtowels, socks, or child's underwear

Water is an element that young children love, and it relaxes them so they can focus longer on the task. Put your child into a comfortable position at the sink or outside at a table and work together to mix a basin of warm soapy water. Show your child how to scrub out the spots and then wring them out and set them aside. Repeat with rinse water and hang to dry.

Extensions:

- If your child resists bath time, bring the pieces of laundry into the tub.
- Let your child wash clothes from a doll or stuffed animal.
- Make a small clothesline and let your child hang the clothes out to dry, using non-spring clothespins.

Wish List

Time: 5 to 10 minutes

Materials: Pad of paper, pen

When your child wants something at a store, take out the paper and write it down together. Knowing that you are listening can go a long way toward eliminating crying or tantrums.

Extensions:

- Use the list for rewards for especially good or loving behavior.
- Put the list where your child can see it and ask you to read it.
- Cross out each wish that is granted so your child can look back on all that they have.

Bedtime Race

Time: 15 minutes

Materials: Small timer

Preschoolers love a challenge, and you can use that to your advantage at bedtime. Set a small timer for 15 minutes as a signal for your child to run for the bedroom, change clothes, brush her teeth, and hop into bed. Your child wins if the timer has not gone off. Follow with a favorite storybook.

Extension:

- If you have troubles with story time, set the timer and begin where you left off with any unfinished books the next night.

Celebration Count-Down

Time: 25 to 30 minutes

Materials: Colored paper, glue

Using visuals tools to help your child look forward to special days can help to control anticipation. Make a paper link chain that corresponds to the number of days until the special day. Hang it in a prominent place chosen by your child and remove one link every night at bedtime.

Extensions:

- Make a chain from pieces of wrapped candy.
- If you are away on a trip, make a chain with small (inexpensive) gifts for each day you will be gone.

Cereal Counting Game

Time: 15 to 20 minutes

Materials: Dry cereal, empty egg carton, pen

Take an empty egg carton and write a number from 1 to 12 on the inside of each section with a black felt pen. Use a cup of cereal to fill the correct amount in each carton section. Recount when you are finished, eating as you go.

Extensions:

- Use other nonsweet treats like carrot circles, celery slices, strawberries, or raisins.
- Use an empty egg carton to count out 12 pieces, 1 in each section.

Cereal Necklace

Time: 30 minutes

Materials: Piece of yarn cut to fit comfortably around the neck, glue or scotch tape, ring-shaped dry cereal ($)

Use yarn that has been dipped in glue on one end (and allowed to dry ahead of time) or tipped with a piece of scotch tape as you thread. String the cereal pieces together until they form a necklace that can be worn or eaten, and tie off the ends.

Extensions:

- Make bracelets or anklets with elastic thread.
- Wear them out to lunch or on a walk together.

Chores

Time: 15 to 20 minutes

Materials: None

Having regular chores for everyone in the family promotes teamwork and cooperation. Some age-appropriate suggestions could include: pick up trash, empty trash cans, help set the table, sort laundry, feed pets, or put newspapers into bags.

Extensions:

- Have a grab bag of chores listed on slips of paper for your child to pick from.
- Do the above but add dice to roll to see how many slips to choose.
- Include yourself in the draw.

Cooking Math

Time: 15 to 30 minutes

Materials: Simple recipe and the needed ingredients

Cooking is a natural way to focus on and understand fractions. Whenever you are in the kitchen, say things like, "Let's divide the cookie dough into two parts so we can bake some now and cook the other half later."

Extensions:

- Challenge your child to divide a food item for two or three people and guide their thinking process as they try to make them even.
- Let your child use a plastic knife to divide a piece of food into smaller pieces, discussing the results.

Counting Walk

Time: 20 to 30 minutes

Materials: None

The next time you go for a walk together, pick out something to count along the way such as cars, kinds or colors of flowers, birds, etc.

Extensions:

- Write down the things you count as you walk.
- Repeat weekly and see the variations from trip to trip.

Familiar Numbers

Time: 5 to 10 minutes

Materials: Paper, pen or pencil

To make number concepts more interesting, talk about the numbers that matter most to your child, such as his age, address, height, and weight, and the time. Make a list of those numbers to talk about together.

Extensions:

- Take a walk and look for numbers.
- Travel around the house and find all the numbers you can. Which rooms have the most?
- Let your child pick a particular numeral and look just for it.

Find Red

Time: 15 minutes

Materials: Designated room or outside area

Work together to find everything in the room that is a specific color.

Extensions:

- Change the color.
- Change rooms.
- Challenge your child to find a small or large object of that color.
- Play hot or cold as you lead each other to a particular object.
- Hide an object of the chosen color in a room and have your toddler look for it.

Funnel and Fill

Time: 20 to 30 minutes

Materials: Several small funnels, plastic bottles, water

Set out an array of small funnels, cups, and plastic bottles and work together to transfer the water from one bottle to another.

Extensions:

- Pretend you are both making chocolate milk, medicine for a sick doll, or bottles of soda.
- Add plastic tubing that will fit around the point of the funnel and carry the water directly into the container.
- Have a pretend tea party together.
- Mix batches of colored water using food coloring.

Go Fish

Time: 10 to 20 minutes

Materials: Yardstick, string or yarn, small magnet, glue, colored paper, paper clips

Tape piece of yarn 3 to 5 feet long on the end of a yardstick. At the end of the yarn, attach a small magnet with the glue and allow it to dry overnight. Cut colored fish out of the paper and glue a paper clip on each fish, allowing it to dry with the pole. To play, put the fish on the floor and dangle the magnet over the paper clips.

Extensions:

- For an added challenge, pick a subject area that your child is learning (colors, numbers, words) and put the components on each fish so your child can identify them when they are caught.
- Write the names of family members and friends on the fish and give the fish to those people when it is caught.
- Use envelopes instead of paper fish and seal in small pieces of cereal or raisins.

Green in a Bag

Time: 15 to 30 minutes

Materials: 1 cup cornstarch, ⅓ cup sugar, 4 cups water, plastic baggies, blue and yellow food coloring

Mix together the cornstarch, sugar, and water. Fill a closable baggie about ⅓ full with the mixture. Drop in food coloring (yellow and blue) but do not mix. Zip shut so the child can mix the color through the plastic by kneading it with her fingers. This is a gentle and quiet activity, and it is important to avoid rough play since the bags can tear.

Match the Numbers

Time: 15 to 20 minutes

Materials: Old calendar, scissors

Give the child a calendar page with the numbers intact. Cut up the numerals on a second calendar page (that has the same number of days) and match up the numerals, laying the corresponding ones on top of each other.

Extension:

- Go back and mark special days, noting their numbers so you can remember them during the upcoming month.

My Muscles

Time: 20 minutes

Materials: None

This exercise can help your child with muscle control. It begins by running until a signal is heard (bell, command, music stopping, etc.), then freezing for a brief moment, and then melting limply into a heap.

Extension:

- A variation could be done by lying on one side and contracting into a ball, holding that pose and extending again into a full lying position on command.

My Own Place

Time: 5 to 10 minutes

Materials: Drawer near your home's entrance

Children can become frustrated when they cannot find belongings. To prevent lost items, assign drawers for each of you to store important items like keys, homework, mittens, and other frequently used personal belongings.

Extensions:

- Label and decorate the drawer fronts and cover them with clear contact paper ($), if desired.
- Add small box lids or plastic containers to separate items and keep the drawers organized.

Sand Writing

Time: 20 to 30 minutes

Materials: fine sand ($), funnel, sidewalk or driveway

Fill the funnel with fine sand, covering the opening with the palm of the hand. Move close to the hard surface and remove the hand, using the movement of the funnel to "write" names, designs, etc. Sweep into a pile and recycle to do again.

Extensions:

- Add funnels of differing sizes.
- Use some colored sand to add highlights and details.
- Have several people begin together with a repeated simple motion in parallel lines.

Scavenger Number Hunt

Time: 20 to 30 minutes

Materials: Common household and food items, paper, pen

Search through the house and make a list of common objects that have numbers printed on them.

Extensions:

- Arrange the items in order from the smallest to the largest number. Examples of items might be: 3 Musketeers, V8 juice, 9 Lives cat food, Ajax 2, VO5, 7 UP.
- This hunt can also be done in the grocery store while shopping.

Tight Space

Time: 15 to 20 minutes

Materials: Masking tape or chalk, music

This activity challenges a focus on body mastery and body awareness. Use the tape or chalk to mark off an area about 2- to 3-feet square. Play music and move slowly within the marked area, without crossing the line.

Extensions:

- Use music with different tempos, including some that is very fast.
- When the music stops, freeze.
- Make adjacent shapes so you can move individually.
- Work together within one space.
- Change the size and see what happens to the kinds of movements each of you can do.
- Ask your child to make a space for you.

Trace Around

Time: 10 to 15 minutes

Materials: Variety of round objects that can be traced, pens or pencils, paper

Work together to trace around the lids, cans, etc.

Extensions:

- Cut the circles out and sort them smallest to largest.
- Trace a circular object several times across the page so that the traced circles overlap, forming a design.
- Challenge your child to find more round objects to trace.
- Gather other objects to trace and talk about the resulting shapes.

Walk Backward

Time: 5 to 10 minutes

Materials: None

This activity encourages cooperation. Stand at one end of the yard or in an open area at a park and have your child call you toward them as you walk backward, following their vocal directions. Help your child understand that you need to follow his voice to succeed.

Extensions:

- Reverse roles. Reassurance will go a long way toward helping your child overcome a reluctance of moving into the unknown.
- Repeat the same procedure at a slow run and reverse roles again.

Are We There Yet?

Time: Up to 30 minutes

Materials: Map with the area to be covered on a trip, paper, pen or pencil

Provide your child with a map for the trip, making sure that it includes a mileage guide or other easy way to determine how much space on the map equals a mile. Trace the route you plan to take with a magic marker. During the trip, have your child follow the route and estimate the distance traveled.

Extensions:

- Use a small notebook to keep track of the progress and review it at the end of each day.
- Challenge your child to estimate distances between places, introducing the notion of scale.

Big Flip

Time: 15 to 20 minutes

Materials: Package of 3 x 5–inch index cards ($), pen

Pick a basic shape like a circle or triangle and draw the shape on an index card. Draw the same shape on 12 to 15 more cards, changing the shape slightly in position or size. Put the cards back into a "deck" and hold them tightly on one side and then flip through. The faster the cards are flipped, the more the shape will appear to dance and wiggle.

Extension:

- Work together to draw a simple stick figure that will move across each successive card.

Bike Challenge

Time: 20 to 30 minutes

Materials: Scooters, bikes, and other vehicles ($), chalk

Draw an obstacle course to ride through and around.

Extensions:

- With more than one child, have participants begin together at one line and finish together at another, emphasizing control of speed and cooperation.
- Use cones or other objects instead of chalk lines.
- Start in small groups at opposite ends of the course and ride past each other slowly without touching or bumping.
- Assign a safe stopping place and have each child take a turn riding around the area and return to a spot to get off for the next person's turn.
- Be a traffic director and have them follow your arm movements.

Clipboard Fun

Time: 15 to 20 minutes

Materials: Clipboard, paper, pen or pencil

A clipboard is a very grownup tool, so it can make your child feel mature and important. Assign an inventory task, such as tallying the contents of a kitchen or linen cupboard.

Extensions:

- Hang a clipboard by the door with chores listed so your child can use it to check off tasks as they are finished, adding notes about what happened.
- Take clipboards and head out on an alphabet scavenger hunt, finding an item for each letter of the alphabet. Exchange and check for accuracy when finished.
- List questions that you make up together and send your child to interview a family member or friend.

Cookie Paleontologist

Time: 30 minutes

Materials: A few chocolate chip cookies, plastic knife, toothpicks, shellfish or nut pick, small paintbrush

This is a great project to show kids how much patience it takes to be a paleontologist or archeologist. Take a chocolate chip cookie and scrape out as many whole chips as possible. Concentration is required to extract the chips, which are then eaten as a reward.

Extensions:

- Record the number of chips in each cookie and compare results.
- Determine which tools work best to complete the task.

Crazy Dots

Time: 15 to 20 minutes

Materials: Paper, pencil or pen

Each of you place 15 to 20 dots on the surface of a paper so that they are easy to see and spread apart. Exchange papers and look hard at the dots to imagine a picture. Connect the dots so that the picture emerges. If you are stumped, try turning the paper longways. Return the papers when you are finished.

Extensions:

- Increase or reduce the number of dots before exchanging.
- Use the dots to create an interesting face.
- Count the steps from the kitchen to the bedroom and make a map using the dots for steps. Test out the map.

Double or Nothing

Time: 15 to 30 minutes

Materials: Pair of dice, paper, pen or pencil

Use the dice to try to roll doubles, keeping tally of how many throws it takes to do so.

Extensions:

- Use four dice to reach doubles and double-doubles, a much more difficult goal.
- Let your child pick his favorite number and see how many rolls it takes to roll it 5 times.

Fancy Footwork

Time: 10 to 20 minutes

Materials: Paper, masking tape, pen or pencil

Hold the writing tool between the toes instead of the fingers and draw on paper that has been taped to the floor.

Extensions:

- Hang a large piece of paper on the wall and try drawing on it while lying down.
- Work together on a single paper.
- Add music to the task and see if it changes the approach.

Fantasy Jars

Time: 20 to 30 minutes

Materials: Clean, empty glass jars, simple clip art or cartoon figures, acrylic paint ($), a few small brushes, masking tape

Tape the clip art to the inside of the jar so that it faces out. Paint the jar, following the lines of the clip art. Let dry. Remove the clip art. These make wonderful gift and decorator items.

Extensions:

- Sprinkle the wet paint with glitter ($).
- Use additional colors to fill in the blank spaces.

Flowing Art

Time: 15 to 20 minutes

Materials: Long piece of butcher paper, pens or crayons, masking tape, music

Tape the ends of the paper to the table using masking tape and play various types of music (classical, jazz, marching). Walk around the table, coloring to the music as you move.

Extensions:

- Do this with paints and long paintbrushes.
- Use blindfolds while working.

Follow a Recipe

Time: 30 minutes to 1 hour

Materials: Simple recipe, ingredients, cooking utensils

Cooking is a new skill that requires careful attention. Pick a simple recipe together and make a shopping list. As you cook, talk about nutrition, measuring, and cooking methods. Eat, share, and enjoy the final product.

Extensions:

- Let your child handle produce and assist you with value-comparison shopping.
- When you get home, let your child wash produce with a soft brush and do any simple chopping or cutting.
- Use a recipe that you have enjoyed at a family gathering but not cooked together.
- Cook something that one of you doesn't particularly like. Adapt in any way that will improve it for you.

Giant Dominos

Time: 20 to 30 minutes

Materials: As many shoe boxes as possible

Concentration is the name of the game with this activity, as you plan and carefully execute the "domino" set up. Tape the box tops to the box bottoms and place each box upright in front of another box about 6 inches apart from one another. When ready, give the last box a little nudge and stand back to enjoy the chain reaction.

Extensions:

- Start the dominos from two ends and see where they meet.
- Count to see how long it takes and compare over 6 test runs.

Go Blank

Time: 10 to 15 minutes

Materials: None

Begin with 1 person naming a category such as birds, flowers, countries, birds, etc. and the other answering with an example. Then switch roles. The exchange might go something like this: birds—blue jay, flowers—daisy, etc. The game ends when a player cannot think of an answer to the other person's category challenge.

Extension:

- Play the game with both people answering the same category until someone cannot think of an answer. The last person with an answer gets to name the next category.

I Can Help

Time: 15 to 20 minutes

Materials: None

Helping out and being part of the family unit really happens when children help out on a regular basis with household tasks. You can begin by working side by side as children learn the skills required to perform any of the following: sweep floors, make simple lunches, rake leaves, walk dogs, vacuum, help with supervised cooking.

Extensions:

- Assign a chore to each other.
- Make a list of chores and pick one for each day of the next week. Compare how each of you does.
- Divide the above list according to agreed upon fairness; for example, 1 difficult task equals 2 easy ones.

Lean and Leave

Time: 5 to 10 minutes

Materials: None

The object of the game is for one of you to look as if you're leaning on the other, while you are actually standing without support. Begin by leaning onto the other person's shoulder and then shift your weight slightly so that you are actually standing alone. Tell the other player when you are ready for them to walk away.

Extension:

- If you have 3 people, try 2 people leaning into the third with the third leaving when signaled to do so.

Measure Up

Time: 20 to 30 minutes

Materials: Containers such as milk cartons (with the tops cut off), yogurt cups, juice cans, pie tins, etc., water

Choose one of the containers and have your child fill it with water. Ask the child to move the contents to another container and see if the second container is full, overflowing, or partly full. Have your child estimate how the next container will "measure up."

Extensions:

- Arrange the containers from the one that holds the most to the one that holds the least. This activity introduces the concepts of comparing and estimating in a visual way without having to worry about real numbers.
- Pick the largest container and guess how many of each of the others it will take to fill it to the top. Check to see if your guesses are right.

Organize It

Time: 15 to 20 minutes

Materials: None

Pick an area such as a drawer or closet that belongs to your child. Plan how it might be better organized and make decisions, reflecting on various alternatives. Then clean and rearrange it together.

Extension:

- Let your child organize a drawer that belongs to you. Have him ask the necessary questions to get it done well.

Pace and Count

Time: 20 to 30 minutes

Materials: Paper, pen or pencil

In this game, pacing is the purpose, not a way to kill time. Use a pencil and paper to measure and record distances around the house in steps. Examples might be steps to the mailbox, to the front door, to the corner, etc.

Extensions:

- Explore the neighborhood in the same way.
- Buy inexpensive pedometers ($) and measure how far you both go in a set amount of time.
- Chart several days, striving to increase the steps while talking about the benefits of exercise.

Pay the Bill

Time: 5 to 10 minutes

Materials: The bill for dinner out at a restaurant, money to pay it

The next time you are out to eat, let your child review the bill, count out the money, and pay the bill.

Extensions:

- Teach your child how to round numbers and help her determine the general amount of the bill before it comes.
- Let your child help you determine how much to tip.

Puzzle-Thon

Time: 20 to 30 minutes at a time

Materials: 50- to 100-piece jigsaw puzzle

Work on a surface that is protected from traffic and where the project can be left undisturbed over several days.

Extensions:

- Invite others to participate and help out.
- Celebrate with all participants when the puzzle is finished.
- Designate a certain time of the day or day of the week to work on it together.
- Add music and a healthy snack to enhance the experience.

Rain Stick

Time: 15 minutes

Materials: Mailing tube with two plastic end caps, 30 to 40 thin nails, South Western pattern contact paper (optional) ($), or crayons and felt pens ($)

Place the nails into the tube and close with the caps. (This toy is not suitable for children under age 3.) Decorate with contact paper or crayons and felt pens, and tip slowly and gently for a relaxing, rain-like sound.

Extensions:

- Make rain sticks of differing sizes to compare the sounds.
- Visit an Indian-goods store and handle a real rain stick and find out how they are made.
- Research together about other native instruments.

Scratch Art

Time: 1 hour

Materials: Heavy white paper or cardboard, crayons, black tempera paint ($), paintbrush ($), liquid hand soap, large paper clip

Color heavily over the paper with crayons, covering its surface completely with a variety of colors. Mix a small amount of the soap with the black paint and cover the surface entirely. Let dry overnight. Use the paper clip to scratch off a drawing so that the colors show through where the black has been removed.

Extension:

- Cut into strips to use as Christmas ornaments or bookmarks.

Search for a Hundred Numbers

Time: 10 to 20 minutes

Materials: Old magazines and newspapers, scissors, paper, glue

Find the numbers 1 through 100 (or a lower number, if desired) together and cut them out and paste them onto a sheet of paper.

Extensions:

- Do the same exercise with the letters of the alphabet.
- Make simple sentences by gluing together words cut from different pages.

Spaghetti Designs

Time: 15 to 20 minutes

Materials: Spaghetti, rubbing alcohol, food coloring, cardboard or paper plates

Cook the spaghetti, drain, and add ¼ cup of rubbing alcohol to keep it from sticking together. Divide into smaller bowls and add a few drops of food coloring to each, stirring to distribute. Arrange in a design on cardboard or a paper plate. It will stick because of the starch content.

Extensions:

- Draw a picture on the plate or cardboard and outline and fill in with the colored spaghetti.
- Make free-form designs with no pattern or picture.

Spare Change

Time: 15 to 20 minutes

Materials: Pennies, nickels and dimes, pair of dice

By using spare change, you can foster money awareness as well as concentration. Take turns rolling one die. With each roll, a player collects the number of pennies that they rolled on the die. As 5 pennies are collected, the player can turn them in for a nickel. Nickels are turned into dimes, etc. The player reaching a predetermined amount first wins.

Extensions:

- With an older child, increase the total amount needed to win.
- Add quarters and dollar bills to the mix.

Tinker-Peas

Time: 15 to 20 minutes

Materials: Frozen peas, toothpicks

Use peas and toothpicks just like tinker-toys to create mini-sculptures by connecting the peas with toothpicks. Allow to dry and harden.

Extensions:

- Spray paint or varnish the product.
- Add miniature marshmallows.

Touch and Tell

Time: 10 to 15 minutes

Materials: Any room in the house

The first person stands up and walks over and touches something. The next person goes over and touches that object and then another. Any number of people can play, continuing until no one can complete the sequence.

Extensions:

- For a more active version, take this game outside.
- Play the game by touching body parts.

7 curiosity

The desire to learn is present and active from the earliest moments of life. Young children spend each waking moment learning about their world, exploring everything that they can get their hands on. They manage to find things we have long since forgotten, or have at least forgotten to notice.

Children keep us on our toes from morning to night. And why not? Never again will the world be so full of wonder and surprise. Everything begs to be touched, investigated, and understood, with no detail too small to ignore. The drive to explore pushes the limits of safety, time, and order as one mess is left behind in the making of another. Truly, the young child's endless energy can sometimes wear us down.

The activities in this chapter are strategies to keep curiosity alive in acceptable ways. They are designed to keep your child's spirit of investigation and wonder active while modeling acceptable ways to make messes, take things apart, and enjoy the natural abundance and complexity of the world. By working closely with young children, we can help them to appreciate how to slow down, look, and talk in order to see and experience things more fully. With a little foresight and planning, you can fully engage your child in meaningful activities in ways that you can enjoy together.

As you hone curiosity into a pleasurable pastime, creativity and critical thinking will blossom. Give your child the freedom of curiosity and you will add a spark of joy to life that works now and well into the future.

Card Shark

Time: 5 to 10 minutes

Materials: Deck of playing cards

This will be a little messy and you might lose a few cards, but if you are willing to shuffle the deck and hand it over, curiosity will take care of the rest.

Extensions:

- Shuffle the cards and deal them, saying, "One for me and one for you."
- Encourage your baby to give you some cards, being willing to return them if requested.
- Add a few shoe boxes and show your baby how to put cards into them.
- Put cards in your pockets and let your baby retrieve them.

Change It

Time: 5 to 10 minutes

Materials: Cupboard with safe items that can be removed

To engender curiosity and safe exploration, make it a habit to put heavy breakable items in overhead cabinets and safe objects in the lower ones and encourage rummaging through them. Good low level candidates include pots and pans, cookie sheets, small canned goods, bottled items, paper bags and small boxes, potatoes.

Extension:

- Surprise your baby by hiding a few animal crackers or a small cup of dry cereal in the cupboard.

Echo

Time: 5 to 10 minutes

Materials: Mailbox

While you are out on a walk, stop at your mailbox, lift up your baby, and as you open the lid, shout inside. The echo is terrific and will bring surprised looks and more calling and echoes. It is likely that this will become a favorite destination for walks.

Extensions:

- Take turns hollering into the mailbox.
- Sing a simple song into it.

Icebergs

Time: 15 to 20 minutes

Materials: Empty half-gallon milk carton, hand-sized plastic objects, shallow baking dish

This puzzling activity can provide interest on and off for up to an hour. Put some small plastic objects into an empty milk carton and fill it 3/4 full with water. Freeze over night. When you are ready to play, run warm water over the carton to peel it off and place the ice block in a shallow baking dish outside. When melted, the toys will be set free.

Extensions:

- Instead of toys, add some grapes or strawberries before freezing.
- Put the frozen cube into a wading pool during water play.

Metal Melody

Time: 5 to 10 minutes

Materials: Large metal cooking pot, safe small household objects

Babies are often startled by noises, and with this activity your baby can control the timing. Experiment together by dropping the hand-sized objects into the pot.

Extensions:

- Hold the items up higher and drop them in.
- Shake the pan and let them rattle for a different sound.
- Add a lid and shake the pot.
- Turn the pot over and drop the objects on the back side.
- Small wooden table blocks ($) work well for this activity.

Reach and Splash

Time: 5 to 10 minutes

Materials: Empty aluminum pie tin, water

The properties of water are fun to discover. Pour an inch of water in the pie tin. Place it just within your baby's reach and watch the fun begin.

Extensions:

- Use warm water to surprise your baby.
- Offer a sponge or small washcloth, squeezing the water out by holding it high so the water falls down.
- Add a little bubble bath, food coloring or scented extract.
- Add floating rubber toys ($) that can be easily grabbed.

Rolling Baby Book

Time: 5 to 10 minutes

Materials: Round empty oatmeal box; bright, simple pictures of animals and common objects, glue, clear contact paper (optional) ($)

As the box rolls and new pictures come into view, your baby will be enticed to see which picture comes next. Glue the pictures onto the empty oatmeal container and let dry. Cover with clear contact paper, if desired. This makes an interesting toy to talk about as you play together.

Extensions:

- Ask your baby to identify a particular picture.
- Glue on pictures of family members and challenge your baby to find someone.

Sounds Around

Time: 5 to 10 minutes

Materials: None

With so many sounds around, curiosity can be aroused by simply drawing attention to them. Good opportunities include when you are using small appliances like mixing and washing machines, vacuum cleaners, toasters, kitchen timers or doorbells, or toilets.

Extensions:

- If safe, let your baby touch such noisemakers as the washing machine, hair dryer, or a flushing toilet.
- Hold your baby up to take a turn pushing the doorbell.

Sticky Fun

Time: 5 to 10 minutes

Materials: Duct tape, hand-sized objects, a sheet of contact paper about 2 feet long ($)

This activity will surprise and mystify your baby. Lay the contact paper out on the floor sticky-side up and tape it down around the edges with duct tape. Place the objects on it and lift them off together.

Extensions:

- Gently place your baby's palm down on the sticky surface.
- Repeat with bare feet.
- If your baby can eat pieces of dry cereal, add a few pieces to the sticky side.
- Tape the paper sticky-side out on the wall.

Texture Crawl

Time: 5 to 10 minutes

Materials: Safe articles with interesting textures, such as a rubber floor mat, carpet samples, silk scarves, chenille rug, bubble wrap, a piece of corduroy, velvet, satin, sticky side of a piece of contact paper, etc.

Your crawling baby will love feeling these interesting articles if you scatter them across the floor. Get down on the floor and explore them together, using words like *cool*, *smooth*, and *bumpy* to talk about what you feel.

Extensions:

- Demonstrate how to feel them with the face or feet.
- If your baby can stand against a low table, put some of the objects on top for feeling from a different angle.
- Float a sheer scarf over your baby's face.
- Put some of the objects in a box and help your baby to pull them out.

Touch Tour

Time: 5 to 10 minutes

Materials: Safe common household items

Treat your baby to a bird's eye view of the world and a chance to touch things too high to reach. Carry your baby around at your eye level and name each object as you touch it. Include things like wall hangings, raised letters, doorbells, and stone or brickwork.

Extensions:

- Take this game outdoors and find new candidates to touch.
- Move up to a sink and feel cool and slightly warm water.
- Open the freezer and touch cold things with the tip of the finger.

Unwrap It

Time: 10 to 15 minutes

Materials: Empty box wrapped in paper

Babies love to unwrap boxes, and you can cater to that joyful activity by wrapping a few to be torn open.

Extensions:

- Enclose small favorite belongings like blankets, books, or toys.
- Substitute the newspaper comics for wrapping paper.
- Wrap a few pieces of cereal or crackers inside.

Water Swing

Time: 10 to 20 minutes

Materials: Lawn sprinkler, toddler seat swing ($)

Turn on an oscillating sprinkler that has been up near a swing so the drops fall on the baby as he swings back and forth. This activity should bring squeals of interest and delight.

Extensions:

- Hold your baby and run in and out of the sprinkler.
- Go through the sprinkler with an umbrella.

Apple Hunt

Time: 15 to 20 minutes

Materials: Foods made with apples, such as breads, pies, sauces, fresh fruit, dried fruit

Young children love to explore new foods by touching and tasting, and because apples are always a favorite, it can be fun to explore together some of the ways we can eat them. Offer a variety of small pieces and talk about them as you taste together.

Extensions:

- Make some of the apple foods together, such as applesauce or baked apples.
- Take turns hiding apples and finding them.
- Peel and cut small pieces of apples and have an apple and tea party.

Backyard Mysteries

Time: 15 to 20 minutes

Materials: Bag or basket for collecting

The outdoors is a wonderful place for exploring and discovering when you are a toddler. Take a container outside and fill it with rocks, twigs, leaves, and pinecones that you and your toddler find together. Dump them out and talk about what you have collected.

Extensions:

- You can extend the activity by asking your toddler to find and pass a specific item to you.
- Make a collage by gluing the items onto cardboard or paper to hang for all to see.

Basic Bubbles

Time: 20 minutes

Materials: 2 cups liquid dishwashing detergent, 6 cups of water, ¾ cup of corn syrup ($)

Bubbles are always mysterious and fun. Combine the ingredients and use a small bubble wand to show your toddler how to blow bubbles. Make sure to keep hands out of the bubble mixture, as it will burn eyes.

Boat Races

Time: 15 to 20 minutes

Materials: Bathtub full of water, small toys that float, disposable foil baking pans ($)

You will have fun learning how much you can put into these shiny boats before they tip over. Put the foil pans into the bath water and show your toddler how to put small bath toys into the boats and give them a ride.

Extensions:

- This activity is great when taken outdoors to the wading pool.
- Use a cup to fill the boat with water.
- Link several boats together with paper clips. (Dispose of the paper clips when finished.)

Cold Finger Paint

Time: 10 to 15 minutes

Materials: Paper, small amount of finger paint that has been chilled in the refrigerator ($)

You will see the curious look of surprise on your toddler's face when you do this activity together. Dab some cold finger paint on the paper to spread with the fingers for an interesting experience as the warm hands meet the cold paint. Talk about the feelings you both get.

Extensions:

- Freeze the paint in an ice cube tray so you can slide the cubes around on paper.
- Add a squirt of shaving cream when the cold paint has warmed up and mix it in with your fingers.

Dip It

Time: 5 to 10 minutes

Materials: Healthy finger foods

Dipping foods changes a toddler's taste and excites curiosity, and by offering healthy dips, you can make a little snack go a long way toward providing good nutrition. Dips can include such healthy choices as yogurt, cheese sauce, pureed chickpeas, fruits or vegetables, and cottage cheese.

Extensions:

- Offer 2 dips so your toddler can experiment and choose.
- Add food coloring for a festive look.

Floor Art

Time: 15 to 20 minutes

Materials: Large piece of paper taped to the floor, crayons, or felt pens ($), masking tape

This activity allows your toddler to experience an entirely new dimension in scribbling by using the whole body, instead of just the arm, to move around the paper. Tape the large piece of paper to the floor and begin to draw together, moving about as needed.

Extensions:

- Cut several pieces of butcher paper into basic shapes (circle, triangle, square, etc.). Tape the edges down completely with masking tape and draw on them.
- Take this activity outside to a sidewalk or driveway substituting chalk ($).

Giant Ballpoint Pen

Time: 10 to 15 minutes

Materials: Paper, empty roll-on deodorant bottles, thinned tempera paint ($)

This activity provides a whole new experience with drawing tools. Pry off the bottle lids and wash the parts thoroughly. Fill the bottles with the thinned paints, replace the tops, and use it to draw on paper. This makes a giant and easy-to-hold "ballpoint" art pen that your toddler can handle easily.

Extensions:

- Hang paper on a wall and cover the floor beneath it with newspaper so your toddler can draw standing up.
- Tape paper to the floor and color from a kneeling position.

Magic Gelatin

Time: 10 to 15 minutes

Materials: Package of lemon gelatin ($), red or blue food coloring ($)

A surprise is in store when your toddler helps you with this gelatin recipe. Freeze water that has been colored and add the colored cubes to the gelatin during preparation, following package directions for using ice instead of water. Use red cubes to make the gelatin orange and blue cubes to make it green. Talk about what happens as the colors change.

Extensions:

- Divide the lemon gelatin into three bowls so you can leave some yellow and turn the other servings orange and green. Let set and spoon into dishes for a rainbow treat.
- Find fruit that matches the color of gelatin and add it to the mix before it sets.

Paper Play

Time: 5 to 10 minutes

Materials: Box filled with as many kinds of paper as you can find, such as magazine pages, wax paper, telephone books, tissue paper, junk mail, catalogues, wrapping paper

This activity will delight and excite your toddler and is well worth the mess. Open the box filled with papers and set it down, taking your cues from your toddler as you play together with it.

Extensions:

- Show your toddler how to rip paper.
- Crinkle the papers into balls to toss about the room.
- Spread the papers out and walk across the pieces carefully.
- Tear a hole and place a paper on your head for a floppy hat.
- Use a hole to play peekaboo together.

Reach for It

Time: 10 to 15 minutes

Materials: Hand-sized household objects

Busy toddlers have to listen to the word *no* all day. You can create a surprise for your toddler by putting safe things out that can be handled in places where they would not ordinarily be found. Interesting options could include a deck of cards, a wallet, jewelry, brightly colored adult socks, a music box, a cup with cereal.

Extension:

- Add safe items to drawers and toy boxes and help your toddler discover them.

Reach Inside

Time: 5 to 10 minutes

Materials: Small plastic jar, grapes

This seemingly simple task presents a challenge as your toddler explores and problem-solves. Fill the jar high enough with grapes so your toddler can reach in and pull them out to eat or play with.

Extensions:

- Offer a plastic bowl to dump the contents into.
- Fill the jar with cereal pieces or little fish crackers.

Rock Walk

Time: 20 minutes

Materials: Basket

Rocks are so different and beautiful once you start looking closely for them. Take a walk together and pick up only rocks, saving them in the basket to carry home.

Extensions:

- Use a bucket of soapy water and a scrub brush to clean them when you get home.
- Help your toddler make a display of the cleaned rocks to share with other friends and family members.
- Paint the rocks different colors, perhaps adding faces.
- Find a space outdoors and make a rock "garden."

Simple Tearing

Time: 5 to 15 minutes

Materials: Newspaper

This activity involves touch, sound, and sight in a fun way. Take a piece of newspaper and tear it up slowly and then vigorously.

Extensions:

- Toss the torn pieces into the air for an impromptu celebration.
- Tear carefully into specific shapes: a star, ball, or heart.
- Add different kinds of paper and use words like *easier* and *harder* as you tear them.

Tabletop Water-Play

Time: 20 to 30 minutes

Materials: Large and small plastic bowl, large plastic cooking spoon, water

The motion and properties of water are mysteries to toddlers, and exploring them can provide great entertainment. Sit with your toddler at a low table outside and demonstrate how to spoon water from the big bowl to the little bowl.

Extensions:

- Add ice cubes to make it more challenging.
- Float a few grapes in the water for spooning and eating.

Balloon Magic

Time: 5 to 10 minutes

Materials: Balloons

Your young child is learning about gravity from trial and error. This activity challenges those emerging concepts with unexpected variations. Blow up a few balloons and tie them off. Rub each one on a wool carpet, sweater, or fur until enough electricity is generated so that when they are placed on the wall, they stick like magic. Note: dispose of all broken balloons immediately, as they pose a serious choke hazard.

Extensions:

- When the balloon is electrified, it can be used to attract and lift your hair.
- Blow up balloons of different colors and stick them to the wall in similar groupings.
- Inflate them so that some are larger and sort onto the wall by size.

Color Mix

Time: 15 to 20 minutes

Materials: Half a dozen small bowls; measuring cups; apron or old shirt; red, yellow, and blue food coloring ($)

Surprise discoveries are in store with this activity, and the results will be different each time. Have your child wear an apron so she can concentrate on the process instead of trying to keep the colors off clothing. Fill three of the bowls with water and color one red, one blue, and one yellow. Use the measuring cups to add and move colors to discover which new colors are created. Talk about what is happening and suggest other ways to mix, if needed. When the water becomes brownish, rinse everything out and begin again.

This is an excellent outdoor activity on a nice day.

Extension:

- Use a small paintbrush ($) to paint a swatch of each color you make on a white piece of paper so you can review all the different colors and shades you created together.

Drip Painting

Time: 20 to 30 minutes

Materials: Large pieces of paper, drop cloth, or newspapers; tempera paint ($); medium-sized paintbrushes ($)

This is best done outside, but can be done indoors if a large drop cloth or newspapers are used to protect the floor. Have your child dip the brush into the paint and drip it onto the paper instead of brushing it on.

Extensions:

- Cut the paper into a shape like a fish or flower.
- Drip white paint on black paper ($) or black paint on white paper for a vivid effect.

Grassworks

Time: 5 to 10 minutes

Materials: Piece of heavy fabric cut at least 1 foot square, toothpicks

This activity lets you demonstrate photosynthesis to your young child in a way that is wonderfully concrete. Cut out the first letter in your child's name from the fabric and pin it to the lawn with toothpicks. Let it stay in place for several days to a week, depending on the amount of sunshine it can be exposed to. When it is removed, the letter will show up on the grass as the chlorophyll is decreased from lack of sunshine.

Extension:

- Make a simple design or a face with fabric scraps.

Handful Scribble

Time: 15 to 20 minutes

Materials: Handful of crayon pieces that are about the same length, rubber band, large piece of white paper, masking tape

Tape the paper to the table to keep it from slipping. Bundle the crayons together with the rubber band, making sure that the tips are all as even as possible. Work together as you cover the paper with bundles of color.

Extensions:

- Play different kinds of music while you work.
- Use larger and then smaller paper.
- Try using bundled colored-chalk outside.

Hidden Prizes

Time: 10 to 15 minutes

Materials: Plastic tub full of sand, small metal objects, magnet ($)

A magnet is fun to play with, and in this activity it is paired with the excitement of a treasure hunt. Hide the metal objects in the sand and let your child pull them out with the magnet.

Extensions:

- Make a list of each item in the sand to cross off as they are pulled out until all are found.
- Add a few plastic items and discuss what happens to them.
- Have your child gather a few items around the house and try them out, and then discuss the results.

Light to Dark

Time: 5 to 10 minutes

Materials: Clear glass of water, food coloring ($)

Exploring color helps young children learn about their environment and all of its subtleties. Put a single drop of color into the water and stir. Talk about the color you see. Continue adding a drop at a time so your child can see the difference in shades from light to dark. Use words to help your child describe what is happening.

Extension:

- Find samples of colors from fabrics or magazine pictures and talk about whether they are dark or light.

Magic Celery

Time: 5 to 10 minutes

Materials: Celery stalks, clean jars, food coloring ($)

Celery stalks take on beautiful flower-like colors when you place them stem down into jars of colored water about an inch deep. Leave several hours or overnight.

Extensions:

- For a rainbow effect, add several colors, one at a time, waiting several hours in between.
- For a special treat, buy some white or light-colored carnations ($) and color them with the same process.

Marshmallow Magic

Time: 15 to 20 minutes

Materials: Dark paper, white glue, saucer, miniature marshmallows ($)

The stark contrast of black and white makes the use of space all the more obvious to the developing artist. Pour a small amount of glue into a saucer and show your child how to dip a marshmallow in and stick it in patterns to the dark paper. Young children are apt to put them all in one spot, and that is fine.

Extensions:

- Make little snowmen by gluing the marshmallows 3 high.
- Take turns gluing marshmallows in a long line.
- Go just around the edges of the paper with marshmallows.

Musical Art

Time: 10 to 30 minutes

Materials: Felt pens ($), large pieces of paper, music

Music can add a new dimension to any art activity. In this case, some soft and slow music is used to set the mood as you both sit down and draw with colored felt pens on large drawing paper and let the mind and pens wander with the sounds.

Extensions:

- Switch to marching band or jazz music.
- Move the paper down to the floor.

Painted Jars

Time: 20 to 30 minutes

Materials: Washed and dried glass jars with lids, tempera paint ($), paintbrush ($)

The joy of creative discovery happens quickly when colors are mixed as they drip and run together on the outside of the jars. Use one or two colors to decorate the glass. Good combinations include red and yellow or blue and yellow. Allow the jars to dry thoroughly and use them to store little items like hair clips or baseball cards.

Plant Facts

Time: 5 to 10 minutes of preparation

Materials: 2 small similar potted plants

This activity teaches your child that sunshine is needed for healthy plants. Put one plant on a windowsill and another in a closet. Continue to water both, and look at them every few days to compare the results. Talk about how sunshine is needed to make plants grow.

Extension:

- Put 2 plants in the sun, but water only one of them, and compare the results. Talk about water as also being a necessary ingredient.

Rainbow Binoculars

Time: 20 to 30 minutes

Materials: Rubber bands, 4 to 6 empty toilet paper rolls, at least 2 colors of clear plastic food wrap cut into 4-inch squares ($)

How different the world looks through these magical colored lenses. Place a colored square of plastic wrap evenly over one end of each roll, holding it in place and pulling it tight with the rubber band. Look through them together, either one or two at a time. Help your child come up with words to describe what is seen.

Extensions:

- Use a different color for each eye and talk about what you see.
- Trade colors and talk about how each one makes you feel as you look at the things around you.
- Tape a 12-inch square of the colored wrap on a window for looking outside.

Rainbow Crayons

Time: 15 to 30 minutes

Materials: Muffin tin, old broken crayons, muffin paper liners ($)

Why settle for coloring with one color when you can have the excitement of using several at a time? Line muffin tins with paper cupcake liners. Put several peeled crayons in the cups until they are about half full. You can mix colors or keep them separate. Preheat oven to 350 degrees and put the tins in for about 10 minutes or until the crayons melt. Remove and let cool before peeling off the paper.

Extensions:

- Make batches with just light or dark colors.
- Make custom crayons with just your favorite colors.
- Make batches with similar colors like pinks and reds.

Special Names, Special People

Time: 5 to 10 minutes

Materials: None

Young children love to hear their full names, and with this activity you help them to understand that everyone has more than one name, even mommies and daddies. Share your full name and those of other family members and talk about anyone who has the same name.

Extensions:

- Make a list of everyone your child knows and see how long the list is.
- Make up a silly song with your child's name in it.
- Make up a silly song that includes other people who are special to you both.

Starch and Tissue Designs

Time: 20 to 30 minutes

Materials: White paper, tissue paper ($), liquid starch ($), ½ to 1 inch paintbrushes ($)

Creativity, color, and design are all part of this art activity, and there is no predicting the outcome as you both experiment with these unfamiliar mediums. Demonstrate how to tear the tissue paper and glue it on the white paper using liquid starch and paintbrushes.

Extensions:

- Demonstrate twisting or wadding small pieces of tissue before gluing.
- Glue flat pieces of tissue onto wax paper ($) for a stained-glass effect.

Starchy Finger Paint

Time: 30 minutes to 1 hour

Materials: Paper, liquid starch ($), powdered tempera paint ($)

No child can resist the feeling and visual effects of playing with finger paint, and you will probably find that you enjoy it too. Pour a small amount of liquid starch onto the paper and sprinkle with tempera powder. Mix with your fingers, being sure to keep the fingers away from the eyes. A slick and shiny paper will work best. You can either purchase commercial finger-paint paper or use pages from a magazine.

Extension:

- Begin with one of the primary colors (red, yellow, or blue) and add a second when it is mixed in so your child can discover making new colors.

Sticky Dots

Time: 20 minutes

Materials: Paper, package of bright-colored self-adhesive dots (found in office supply stores) ($)

Because there is a novelty in the newness of the dots, exploration is guaranteed. No directions are needed. Set out a piece of paper and the adhesive dots and let your child work independently to decide how to place them on the paper.

Extensions:

- Tape a paper to the wall at your child's height so that the dots can be put on from a standing position.
- Draw a line down the center of the paper and challenge your child to put a single color of dots on each side.
- Make faces with the dots on circular cutouts.
- For variety, add felt pens ($) and crayons, but only after you have worked for some time with just the dots.

Taste of Colors

Time: 5 to 10 minutes

Materials: Pineapple or orange juice, green food coloring ($)

Use this activity to help your child explore taste and sight. Pour 2 servings of juice and color one with a drop of green food coloring. Do a taste test to see if they taste the same or different.

Extensions:

- Do a blindfold taste test and compare the results.
- Add more colors and repeat the test with and without a blindfold.

Wooden Unit Blocks

Time: 30 minutes to 1 hour

Materials: Sand paper ($), 2 by 4–inch pine boards to cut into 6-, 9- and 12-inch blocks ($)

Few toys are as durable and able to stir the imagination quite as much as wooden blocks, and this is a low-cost version that works just as well as the purchased sets. Your child will explore concepts of geometry, gravity, shape, and balance by playing with them. Cut the boards into carefully measured pieces as described above and sand lightly so they are smooth to the touch. It is best if blocks can be stored for easy access and sorted by size.

Extensions:

- If you have a jigsaw, add a few arched and triangular pieces.
- Introduce small cars and small plastic animals into the play.

Adventure Walk

Time: 20 to 30 minutes

Materials: None

Why walk on the same old route when you can head out on an adventure designed by your child? Let your child give directions for the route and follow along agreeably.

Extensions:

- Help your child plan the next walk before heading out. Write down her directions to take along.
- Pick your next picnic spot by following your child's directions to take a certain number of steps and turns.
- Ask your child to direct your turns as you drive to familiar destinations.

Bus Trip

Time: Up to several hours

Materials: Map, bus fare ($)

For many children, a trip on a bus is a whole new way to experience their neighborhood and city. Use a local map to pick a destination, and check bus schedules and fares as you plan a short trip. Be sure to keep transfers minimal and have the correct change available.

Extension:

- Look at a bus route map together to help plan your excursion.

Color Lab

Time: 20 to 30 minutes

Materials: Rubber bands, balloons ($), flashlight

Indulge in this curiosity-filled activity by stretching a balloon over a flashlight and fastening it tight with a rubber band. Shine it on a wall or ceiling in a dark room.

Extensions:

- By adding different balloon filters, you can make a variety of secondary colors. Try combining red and yellow or blue and yellow.
- If you have several flashlights, you can shine the colors on the wall and do the color mixing there.
- Use 3 flashlights and 3 different colored balloons. Hold them inside a paper grocery bag with holes cut in the bottom. Aim the holes at the ceiling and move the flashlights inside to create a rainbowlike dance of light and color.

Fancy Containers

Time: 20 to 30 minutes

Materials: Recycled aluminum cans with 1 end open (check for sharp edges), glue, several colors of yarn scraps ($), optional paint and glitter ($)

These beautiful containers have as many uses as you both can think up: desk sets, vases, coin savers. Scrub and dry the cans. Dip the yarn pieces into glue and arrange on the cans. Let dry. Paint and glitter are optional.

Extensions:

- Use the yarn to spell out your names.
- Roll the dry can in paint and use it to paint across paper.

Fly-Swatter Bubbles

Time: 15 to 30 minutes

Materials: ½ cup liquid detergent, ⅓ cup water, clean plastic fly swatter ($)

Your child will be wondering just how many bubbles he can make with this easy activity. Dip a fly swatter in the detergent mixture, and make hundreds of bubbles at a wave.

Glacier in a Bottle

Time: 10 to 15 minutes

Materials: Water, food coloring ($), clear plastic bottles, indelible marker ($)

This activity is science in a bottle as you observe the results of a liquid becoming solid. Mark each bottle with a fill line. Mix food coloring into the water and have your child fill each bottle up to that line. Stand upright in the freezer and observe how the ice expands past the lines.

Extension:

- Let 1 bottle melt to see if it returns to its original volume (line).

Icebergs

Time: 30 minutes

Materials: Food coloring ($), a small plastic tub of water, small balloons ($)

Fill balloons with water that has been colored with 10 drops of food coloring and place them in the freezer. When frozen, peel off the balloon and place the cubes in tubs of water for water play.

Extensions:

- Add 1 or 2 of these colorful icebergs to the bathtub.
- Put 2 different-colored icebergs in a large bowl and check them as they melt and blend into a new color.
- Put 1 iceberg in a cool place and another in the sun or by a heater and compare the melting rates.

Kool-Aid Playdough

Time: 30 to 40 minutes

Materials: 2½ to 3 cups flour, 1 tablespoon of oil, 2 cups boiling water, ½ cup salt, 1 package of Kool-Aid drink mix ($), 1 tablespoon of alum ($)

Working with dough is relaxing and pleasurable to children, but it also draws out curiosity about the properties and possibilities of the pliable material as they handle it. Mix together the above ingredients for a dough with a light appealing color and a nice scent. Use up to 1 cup of additional flour to knead into the dough until it reaches the desired consistency. Store in an airtight container.

Extension:

- Label the storage containers with pictures or drawings of the fruit flavors used.

Magnify It

Time: 15 to 30 minutes

Materials: Common objects, small magnifying glass ($)

Four year olds are curious about everything, and this activity opens up a whole new world to their scrutiny. Begin with a few familiar objects and branch out to textures of walls, furniture, and even dirt. Talk to each other about what you see.

Extensions:

- Move outdoors and take a walk to observe in nature.
- Compare various sizes of print with the magnifying glass. Look for familiar letters.
- Examine your facial features at close range and talk about what you see.

Make a Flood

Time: 15 to 20 minutes

Materials: Small jars, bowls, coins

The curiosity built into this activity also draws on planning, observation, and math skills. Place the empty jars in bowls (to keep the water from running all over), and fill them with water to differing levels. Drop coins into the jars one at a time to see the water rise. Count and chart how many coins it takes to make the water overflow.

Extensions:

- Begin again with larger items and try to predict when the overflow will take place.
- Fill two identical jars to the same level and compare the results of putting in a large item in one and small items in the other.

Minimuseum

Time: 15 to 20 minutes

Materials: Low shelf or counter space

Four year olds love to collect just about anything, and sharing discoveries with others engenders a lifelong love of learning. You can help by providing a reachable, central space for the display of whatever your child collects or finds interesting. Talk about the display and share it with others.

Extensions:

- Set paper and pencil by the display so family members can leave comments and questions.
- Bring part of the collection to the dinner table and talk about it while everyone eats.
- Ask a question about the display that requires research and help the child find the answers.

Mud and Rocks

Time: 30 to 40 minutes

Materials: Cleared outdoor spot with dirt, small rocks, small shovel or hand trowel, water hose

The ground may need some preparation, but your child can assist you so that you can get started. Flood the dirt area and excavate it to soften it so that the earth can be easily worked with the hands. Then, let curiosity be your guide as you dig and mold together.

Extensions:

- Add small rocks and use to build castles, moats, dams, bridges, etc.
- Add other natural material like small twigs, leaves, walnut shells.
- Use more water after digging out side pools and waterways.

1 Pound

Time: 5 to 10 minutes

Materials: Grocery items that come packaged in 1-pound weights

Gather together as many items as you can find that weigh 1 pound and compare them by lifting. Show your child where the weight is listed on the package. Examples could include butter, dry beans, popcorn, or coffee.

Extensions:

- Let your child weigh a pound of fruit at the market.
- Weigh your child and talk about how many 1-pound packages would equal his weight.
- Use a small scale ($) to weigh containers of water to see how much a pound is.

Paper Folding

Time: 15 to 20 minutes

Materials: Paper

Manipulating paper to make new shapes encourages creativity and curiosity as you explore how many different ways you can do this activity. Make a paper hat, fold and cut along the folds to make snowflakes, or cut specific shapes like circles or squares. Work together to come up with as many possibilities as you can think of.

Extensions:

- Decorate your creations with paint.
- Add glitter or glue on pieces of ribbon or buttons.
- Make note cards and pair them with envelopes.
- Check out a library book on origami to experiment further with this mode of art.

Powdered-Detergent Finger paint

Time: 30 to 40 minutes

Materials: Powdered laundry detergent, paper, powdered tempera paint ($)

This is another easy-to-make finger paint that brings our creative moods. Mix 5 tablespoons of liquid tempera paint with 1 cup of powdered detergent and 1/4 cup of water, adding the water slowly as needed until the consistency is smooth and creamy. Keep away from the eyes. A little liquid soap can be added to help prevent clothing stains.

Extensions:

- Add scents or extracts.
- Add uncooked rice or oatmeal for an interesting texture.

Rough Going

Time: 10 to 15 minutes

Materials: Sheets of several grades of sandpaper ($), Q-tips ($), any kind of paint ($)

Experiment with various grades of sandpaper by painting on them using Q-tips for paintbrushes.

Extensions:

- Experiment with using crayons and felt pens on sandpaper. Talk about which are easier and why.

Sink and Float

Time: 30 minutes

Materials: Small objects like marbles, paper clips, cork, beads, rocks, sponges, etc., tub of water, paper and pencil

This game of concentration also uses curiosity to promote observations of how gravity and weight work. Fill the tub with water and sit together to test each object to see if it will sink or float. Chart the results in 2 columns. Talk about what you see and learn.

Extensions:

- Gather different objects and try to predict the results before they happen.
- Use this game at bath time by bringing the items into the tub.

Steamed Rice

Time: 20 minutes

Materials: Cooking pot, rice, water, measuring cup

Steaming rice together lets you discover how the rice changes texture and size from the heat and absorption. Let your child help with the measuring, pouring, and watching the time. Add some butter or soy sauce for a healthy snack together when you are finished.

Extension:

- Use the leftover cold rice to make rice pudding.

With or Without Ice

Time: 10 to 15 minutes

Materials: Water, ice, drinking glass, measuring cup

If your child wonders why the drink disappeared so fast, this activity will provide the answer and demonstrate the lost value of a drink that is filled with ice. Fill a glass with ice and pour in water until it is full. Empty the water into a measuring cup. Take the ice out and fill the same glass. Repeat the measuring. Discuss which would be the best value if purchased.

Extension:

- Repeat the experiment with varying amounts of ice.
- Save paper cups from purchased beverages and measure the contents before and after ice is added to see how much you actually got.

Blindfold Painting

Time: 20 to 30 minutes

Materials: White paper, blindfold, paintbrush ($), tempera paint ($)

This activity challenges your child to think in new ways and explore new feelings. Feel the paper to get a clear understanding of where the paint and brushes are before you put on the blindfold and begin. Paint on the surface while blindfolded by focusing on the arm and finger movements. You will both discover the interesting challenges of creating artwork without vision.

Extensions:

- Do the same project using crayons or felt pens with the paper.
- Draw the same picture with eyes open and with the blindfold on and talk about the differences in the process.
- Challenge each other to draw a particular item with the eyes covered.

Bubble Painting

Time: 30 to 45 minutes

Materials: ½ cup of liquid dish detergent, ⅓ cup of water, shallow pan, light-colored paper, newspaper, package of straws ($), food coloring ($)

This activity is a quiet one because of the care and observation required to create magical colored bubbles. Cover the work surface with newspaper before you mix the liquid detergent and the water in a shallow pan. Add a few drops of food coloring. Tip one end of a straw into the pan and lift it up. Blow through the other side to create a bubble and then slowly pick up a piece of light-colored paper and pop the bubble on it. Keep doing this with different colors until there is a great colorful bubble print picture.

Extensions:

- Try this on a smooth piece of scrap lumber.
- Use plain white paper to create gift wrapping.
- Cut into strips and use for bookmarks.

Disassemble

Time: 30 to 40 minutes

Materials: Hand tools such as a wire cutter, screwdriver, or small hammer; an old appliance such as a telephone, toaster, or radio

Your child doesn't need to understand how the appliance works. The fun is in discovering its physical complexity. Work with your child to disassemble the appliance, with the understanding that it does not have to be reassembled. Disassembling, in and of itself, is generally an adequately challenging activity for this age.

Extensions:

- Have your child sort the disassembled parts into piles that are similar in some way.
- If you are able to explain any of the workings, fine. If not, perhaps you can find someone else or a simple book that can lend some explanation to the basic electrical concepts.

Discovery Art Box

Time: 20 to 30 minutes

Materials: Variety of art and craft items, small boxes for storage

Curiosity can be engendered by as simple an act as how you offer and display art and craft supplies. Store art and craft items in individual small boxes so they are ready to use at a moment's notice. Materials could include a stapler, hole punch, ruler, paste, scissors, pipe cleaners, colored pencils, charcoal pencil, facial tissues, paper clips, pinking shears, small tablets, pieces of metallic or origami paper, confetti, seeds, or costume jewelry. Let your imagination be your guide.

Extension:

- Put together a box of stored materials that can be kept and used in the car.

Dry Painting

Time: 20 to 30 minutes

Materials: Paper, water, cotton balls, dry powdered tempera paint ($), paint-brushes ($)

Watching powdered paint spring to life makes this activity a high interest one. Dab dry tempera paint on to the paper with cotton balls and then dip a brush in water and paint over the page to release the colors.

Extension:

- Dab on only 2 colors that will combine to create others, such as red and blue or yellow and blue.

Fall Leaf Prints

Time: 20 to 30 minutes

Materials: Leaves, newspaper, a hammer, 12-inch–square piece of white muslin ($)

This project is very easy to do and creates a highly attractive product that displays your child's interest in nature. Take a walk together to gather leaves, looking for a variety of colors and shapes. Cut a piece of muslin about 12 inches square and place it on a piece of newspaper on a hard work surface. Place a leaf on top and use a hammer to bang gently on the entire leaf surface. Repeat with other leaves on the material and hammer each one completely. Some overlapping is fine. Allow the fabric to dry before brushing off any residue.

Extension:

- Frame or suspend from a dowel and hang on the wall.

Macaroni Skeleton

Time: 30 minutes

Materials: Dark paper, white glue, black felt pen ($), dried lima beans (head, thorax, hips) ($), short macaroni tubes (spine) ($), thick corkscrew macaroni (arms and legs) ($), elbow macaroni (ribs) ($), small shells (joints) ($), spaghetti (fingers and toes) ($)

To prepare for this project, get a book with an illustration of a human skeleton and talk about the even balance between the 2 sides of the body. You may need to make a sample sketch, or even better, sit down with your child and make a model of your own, discussing together where each piece should go. Start at the head, and then do the neck/trunk, and on down. A pen can be used to draw in the eyes and a smile.

Extension:

- Make a skeleton family representing the approximate sizes of the members.

Magic Potion

Time: 10 to 15 minutes

Materials: Coffee mug, water, baking soda, vinegar, cup, saucer

In this simple activity you can stir up the brew that will mystify your child. Put the mug on the saucer in case it bubbles over, and fill it halfway with water. Dissolve 3 tablespoons of baking soda in it. Pour 3 tablespoons of vinegar into a separate cup and add all at once. Bubbles of carbon dioxide are created when the acid in the vinegar reacts with the base in the soda, just as they do in cakes and quick breads, making them rise.

Extensions:

- Make a recipe that calls for baking soda, dividing it into 2 bowls and adding baking soda to only one of them. Cook and compare what the results look like.
- Do a taste test and see if there are differences.

Magnet Sculpture

Time: 15 to 30 minutes

Materials: Bar magnet ($), small paper clips

This activity challenges experience with gravity. Magnetize the clips by rubbing them on the bar in one direction. Once they have acquired a magnetic field, they can be stood end to end vertically, connected horizontally, or moved to form amazing shapes.

Extension:

- See how tall you can make a sculpture.
- Bring the clips out as far as you can horizontally without tipping them over.

Map Facts

Time: 15 to 30 minutes

Materials: Map of the local area

Map skills can develop special concepts that help children understand distance and time. A good way to expose children to maps is to use one of the local area when you take a walk together, following along as you go and planning turns and routes.

Extensions:

- Mark things on the map that are meaningful to either of you, such as where you live or go to school or where friends live. Find a favorite pizza parlor or video store.
- Take a ride to a new place using the map and let your child direct you about turns.
- Graduate to a map of the state to plan an imaginary trip.

Marble Painting

Time: 20 to 30 minutes

Materials: Shoe-box lid, paper, 2 cups, 2 or more colors of tempera paint ($), several marbles ($)

Who would imagine that marbles could provide a painting experience that is so interesting to watch and so fun to do? Cut the paper to fit snugly inside the shoe-box lid. Drop marbles into the cups and add a small amount of tempera paint. Drop each paint-covered marble into the box lid and tip the lid gently so they roll around, leaving trails of paint.

Extensions:

- For Halloween, you can make spider webs by using white paint on black construction paper.
- Use the completed paper as a border for other artwork.
- Use the dried product as unusual gift-wrapping paper.

MEASURE UP

Time: 30 to 40 minutes

Materials: Paper, pencil, ruler, small measuring tape

Young children are fascinated with size, and you can heighten that interest by providing some grown-up measuring tools to compare common household items and record the results. Talk about what is surprising or interesting about the information that you collect together.

Extensions:

- Measure a big object like a car or the perimeter of the house.
- Measure and chart the height of each family member and compare the results.
- Put an empty jar out to collect and measure rain.

MUSICAL BOTTLES

Time: 20 to 30 minutes

Materials: Empty bottles (wine, soda) or tall glasses, spoon

Will more or less water make a deep sound? Can the sounds be combined into a simple song? These are just a few of the questions open for exploration with this simple experiment. Fill the bottles or glasses with different levels of water and tap lightly on each one with a spoon. Talk about the results.

Extensions:

- Make up some short and simple original tunes.
- Work together to tap out a familiar tune like "Happy Birthday."

My Museum

Time: 1 hour

Materials: Collected items

A good way to rouse your child's curiosity is to visit a children's museum that has hands-on exhibits. Afterward, think of a home museum display that you could build together. Provide a safe space where the display can remain undisturbed. Suggestions could include such things as acorns and nuts from a park or seashells from a beach. Invite family and friends to view the results.

Extensions:

- Work together to number and catalogue the items in the collection.
- Create an exhibit that can be touched and handled by visitors.
- Provide materials for visitors to write comments about the exhibit.

Name Game

Time: 5 to 10 minutes

Materials: Paper, pencil

This is a good game if you are waiting at a doctor's office or in line at the bank. Write your names on 2 pieces of paper and see how many words you can make using the letters.

Extensions:

- Add your last names and try again.
- Put your 2 first names together and form words.
- Play this game in the car by using the name of the place you are going to.

Ocean Sounds

Time: 5 to 10 minutes

Materials: Glass, water

Sound waves can mimic the sounds of the ocean. Fill the glass halfway with water and hold it to your child's ear to "hear" the ocean. This happens because the water movement on the side of the glass mimics that of the ocean meeting the sand.

Extension:

- Try other containers and see if the sound can be replicated.

Reverse Painting

Time: 30 minutes

Materials: Bleach, colored tissue paper ($), Q-tips

The unexpected or different challenges curiosity. Be sure to cover up and monitor this activity carefully as bleach can ruin clothing. Select some of the colored tissue paper to work on. Pour some bleach into a shallow cup and dip in one end of a Q-tip. Paint with it on the paper, and watch it remove the color, creating a lovely streaked effect. Allow to dry thoroughly. Rinse any bleach dripped onto the skin immediately with plenty of cool water.

Extension:

- Repeat using dark fabric instead of paper.

Scent-sation

Time: 15 to 30 minutes

Materials: Blindfold, scented foods like lemons, watercress, apples, spices, pretzels, olives, orange slices

Wondering, investigating, and guessing are all part of this challenging activity. Take turns wearing the blindfold as you smell each food and guess what it is.

Extension:

- Repeat this experiment with the eyes covered by tasting and not smelling each food. Does taste work better than smell to make the identification?

Shadow Play

Time: 10 minutes several times a day

Materials: Stick, measuring tape, paper, pencil

Ask your child what people did before watches were invented, and then head outside to make a sundial. In the morning, place the stick in the ground in a sunny spot. Measure the length of the shadow. Repeat every 2 hours, writing down the length of the shadow. Talk about what happened.

Extensions:

- Move the experiment to different locations and see if the results are the same.
- Explore the concepts of sundials and how they were used to tell time.

Shadow Prints

Time: 30 minutes

Materials: Small common household items, black construction paper ($)

Choose a location that will get full sun for the afternoon. Place a piece of black construction paper on the ground and put some small objects on the paper. Leave the items exposed to the sun for the afternoon, and when you remove the items, their outlines will remain. Good subjects include a fork, padlock, key, and small toy.

Extension:

- Help your child check what happened by doing a similar experiment in other parts of the yard with shade, partial-sun, and full sun.

Shining Pennies

Time: 15 to 30 minutes

Materials: Pennies, bottle of vinegar, salt, glass jar with the label removed, paper towels

With a little work, pennies take on a whole new look that will mystify your child. Pour half a cup of vinegar into a clear jar and add 2 tablespoons of salt. Drop in the pennies, one at a time, and watch what happens. Dry with a paper towel to a beautiful shine.

Extension:

- Try this with nickels or dimes and talk about the fact that this particular chemical reaction only works with copper.

Thermometer Fun

Time: 15 to 30 minutes

Materials: Paper, pencil, several outdoor thermometers ($)

The weather affects us in many ways, and your child is learning how to respond to these changes. Place the thermometers in various parts of the yard during the summer or winter (shade and sun) and check and chart them to learn more about these changes. Discuss what is observed and learned.

Extensions:

- Use a thermometer or temperature strip to take your body temperature at different times of the day.
- Run about in the sun and measure if the body temperature changes or remains the same.

Treasure Map

Time: 20 to 30 minutes

Materials: Paper, surprise item, felt pens ($)

Hide a small surprise and draw a map so your child can find it by following the directions. Include specifics such as the number of steps, directions to turn, color of objects involved, etc.

Extensions:

- Let your child make a treasure map for you.
- Work together to make a multi-step treasure hunt for another family member or friend, with new maps and clues at each stop.

8 decision making

We've all known people who are poor decision makers. Their procrastination and muddled thinking can land them anywhere from annoying to downright dangerous. How do people get this way? It is all too likely that no one let them practice making decisions while they were children.

Decision making isn't as natural as having a desire to communicate or a sense of curiosity about the world. It is a skill that must be offered to young children in measured doses so they become comfortable making choices over time. A good place to begin is in the realm of everyday routines, where children can learn that mistakes help them to gain valuable new information.

You can offer your young child large and small choices every day. Should the eggs be scrambled or poached? Will we go to the park or to the library? Which shirt goes with these pants? Practice is where it's at, coupled with your praise and loving encouragement.

The activities in this chapter are designed to encourage your child to express ideas, preferences, and choices within the safe environment of play. As you try them out together, you can model that success feels good and that mistakes are allowed.

Decision-making practice strengthens self-esteem, promotes leadership qualities, and enhances learning. The activities help your child to understand the power and the responsibility inherent in choosing and the pleasure and freedom that results.

Check It Out

Time: 5 to 10 minutes

Materials: Hand-sized safe objects, such as rattles, keys on a ring, measuring spoons, and plastic cups

Babies can make simple decisions as they scoop up common household items to explore with the mouth and hands. Place items into a box or basket and put it within reach, and sit nearby to encourage and share each discovery.

Extensions:

- Put the items into a large kettle with a lid so that your baby can take off the lid and remove the items.
- Sit with your baby and stack several of the items as they are removed, exclaiming playfully when they tip over.
- Say, "Give it to me," as you take each item from your baby. Reverse and give each one back, naming it as you do so.

Choose One

Time: 5 to 10 minutes

Materials: 3 familiar objects

This game requires listening before deciding. Pick up the first object and say its name. Do the same with the others and then ask your baby to pick a particular item. Use its name and repeat your directions until the correct one is chosen.

Climb Aboard

Time: 5 to 10 minutes

Materials: None

By positioning yourself on the floor in a playful position, you invite a decision to participate. While lying on the floor, call your crawling baby to come play with you. Let your baby approach and initiate the rest of the game, such as climbing on top of you.

Extensions:

- Cover your face with a small blanket or pillow and play peekaboo, allowing your baby to remove the cover.
- Say, "Want to go up?" and lift your baby into the air.
- Invite your baby to lie down next to you to giggle and play.

Find the Sound

Time: 5 to 10 minutes

Materials: Masking tape; 3 small, empty milk cartons; 2 kinds of colored contact paper ($); bell ($)

This is a decision game that your baby will love. Put the bell into a carton and seal all 3 cartons securely with masking tape. Cover the 2 empty containers with one kind of contact paper and the bell carton with a different kind. Give your baby the cartons one at a time while shaking them. When you give the carton with the bell, act surprised and pleased when you hear the sound. Help your baby learn to pick the one with the bell.

Extensions:

- Encourage your baby to shake each carton to find the sound.
- Take away the carton with the bell in it and give your baby only the empty ones. See how long play continues before your baby seeks the noisy one.
- Ask your baby to give you the one with the bell and keep asking if the wrong one is offered. Applaud successful choices.

Give It to Me

Time: 5 to 10 minutes

Materials: Common household items or favorite toys

When your baby is playing with something, ask for it and hold out your hand. Your baby might refuse or give it to you and then want it back, either of which is fine.

Extensions:

- When your child is old enough to eat finger foods, ask for a piece and say, "Thank you."
- Hold something of your own and ask, "Do you want this?"

Safe Haven

Time: 5 to 10 minutes

Materials: None

If you are nearby when needed your baby has a chance to choose your comfort. When your baby is unhappy, hold out your arms and ask, "Do you want to come here?" This simple choice offers your baby a tool to help control difficult situations.

Extension:

- Offer a choice of other comfort items, such as a blanket or favorite toy.

String Along

Time: 5 to 10 minutes

Materials: Hand-sized objects, a piece of thick yarn 2 to 3 feet long ($)

Something as simple as grabbing for a toy helps to teach your baby how to control the environment. Tie the object or toy to one end of the piece of yarn and put the other end in your baby's hand. Demonstrate pulling to bring the item closer.

Extensions:

- Toss the toy out and help your baby to pull it back.
- Make several yarn toys so your baby can choose which to pull.
- Sing a song as you swing the toy back and forth toward or above your baby, just close enough that it can be reached.
- When your baby can crawl, pull the toy slowly so it can be followed.
- Use 2 objects and pull them in different directions so your baby can choose which one to follow.

That Makes Three

Time: 5 to 10 minutes

Materials: 3 medium-sized items such as a washrag, yarn ball, small cup, or set of keys

Hand control is still developing, but with this activity you throw in decision making as well. Sit on the floor with your baby and put an object in each hand. Offer a third object, and let your baby figure out how to put down a toy in order to pick up another.

Extensions:

- Ask your baby to give you a toy.
- Put all 3 in front of your baby and don't offer any directions.

What Goes Here?

Time: 5 to 10 minutes

Materials: Hand-sized objects, a muffin tin

This activity is an early game which gives your baby the satisfaction of making decisions. Sit with your baby and put each object into the muffin tin. Ask your baby, "Where can we put this one?" Clap and hug your approval.

Extensions:

- Add a shoe box or a pot with a lid and put an item into it and then close it while your baby watches.
- Hand your baby an object and ask, "Do you want to put it here or there?" indicating two choices. Applaud each decision.
- Take the items out, one at a time, and tell your baby to put them in, demonstrating again, if necessary.
- Turn the muffin tin upside down with the objects out of view and let your baby discover where they are and decide what to do with them.

Beanbag Toss

Time: 5 to 10 minutes

Materials: Large laundry basket, plastic sandwich bags or old socks, package of dry beans ($)

Physical games encourage decision making about when and how to move the body. Tossing objects at a target can give your toddler both pleasure and confidence. Make beanbags to toss by filling plastic sandwich bags (doubled, and sealed with plastic tape) or old socks tied off at the end. Store the bags out of reach when finished.

Extensions:

- Sit across from your toddler with your legs wide open and toss the beanbag back and forth into each other's laps.
- For an easier beginning game, stand over the basket and drop them in.
- Take turns tossing the beanbags into the laundry basket. Help your toddler lift the basket and empty out the beanbags.
- Put your toddler into the laundry basket and toss the bags into her lap.
- Sit across from each other and toss the bags gently back and forth.

Choose a Drink

Time: 5 to 10 minutes

Materials: Plastic drinking cup with lid ($)

Getting toddlers to drink enough liquids is always a challenge, but give your toddler control over the choice, and the task is far easier. Fill the cup with water or juice and leave it where it can be easily reached without your child asking for your assistance.

Extensions:

- Keep a cup of water in the car where your toddler can ask for or reach it.
- Put out a cup with juice and one with water for an additional choice.

Daily Decisions

Time: 5 to 10 minutes

Materials: None

Instead of saying "no," try to find times when you can offer your toddler choices to reduce conflicts and teach decision making. Begin with simple choices like, "Do you want the red cup or the blue one?" "Do you want your eggs scrambled or poached?" "Do you want to color at the table or in the backyard?"

Extensions:

- Try simple choices about food to cut down on mealtime struggles.
- Ask your toddler to choose brushing his teeth before or after his bedtime story.
- At the grocery store, talk about choosing just one treat to carry to the checkout counter

Seek and Find

Time: 15 to 30 minutes

Materials: Brightly colored objects such as scarves, balls, plastic flowers, small pillows, stuffed toys

Surprise your toddler with treasures that can be discovered through a hunt. Hide the objects just far enough or high enough out of sight so that your exploring toddler can discover them with a little exploration. Give hugs and praise with each success.

Extensions:

- Move to another room and hide the objects so you can play again.
- Take the game outside and let the fun begin all over again.
- Hide scarves in your pocket, pant leg, or purse and let your toddler search you for them.

Jingle Toes

Time: 15 to 30 minutes

Materials: Needle and thread, elastic ($), 4 to 6 jingle bells ($)

Your toddler will love to move when motivated by the sound of a jingle bell. Sew 2 or 3 bells onto a strip of elastic that will fit comfortably around each ankle. Stand back and watch the fun begin while your toddler experiments with the sounds and moves about and up and down. Store the bells out of reach. Examine with each use to make sure they cannot come off.

Extensions:

- Add music to speed things up and slow them down.
- Go outdoors where the play can become more vigorous.
- Take a walk around the neighborhood or to the market.
- Challenge your toddler to be noisy and then quiet.
- Put the bells on a favorite stuffed animal.

Pick a Guest

Time: 5 to 10 minutes

Materials: Dolls or stuffed animals

If you have problems getting a toddler to come for dinner or bath, make it a game by asking him to invite along a play guest. Say, "Who is coming to the bath with you?" and help your toddler pick a doll or stuffed animal to bring along.

Potato Fun

Time: 15 to 20 minutes

Materials: Potatoes, cooking oil, milk, seasoning

After your toddler participates in the preparation, choosing will be easier. Prepare potatoes in a number of ways, letting your child help out in simple ways, like pouring or stirring. Do a comparison taste test to see which taste the best. Include possibilities like mashed, fried, baked, boiled, and raw.

Extensions:

- Add a drop of food coloring ($) to one kind and see if that changes the favorite choice.
- Offer ketchup, butter, or sour cream for dipping or adding.
- Serve some potatoes cold and some hot and see which is preferred.

Sticky Business

Time: 10 to 15 minutes

Materials: Masking tape

When your hands are busy or you are on the phone, children can be at their most demanding. Lay out several pieces of tape on the edge of a table and let your toddler experiment with them while you finish your conversation.

Extensions:

- Tell your toddler to move the pieces to a particular destination, such as a low mirror.
- Tell your toddler to put a piece on your nose, ear, hand, etc.
- Tear several pieces a foot or more long and offer them with no directions.
- Show your toddler how to tape a piece of artwork to the wall or refrigerator.
- Playfully tape your mouths shut and mumble together.

Walk or Ride

Time: 5 to 10 minutes

Materials: Stroller or wagon ($)

When you are going on a short outing, offer your arms, walking, or a stroller as the means of moving and see which one your toddler picks.

Extensions:

- Ask your toddler what you can take along to play with in the stroller or in your pocket.
- Put objects into a large paper bag so your toddler can reach in and pull out a surprise as you travel. Exclaim with the name when you both see what it is.
- As you travel, offer a different finger food in each hand and have your toddler choose which one to eat, while you eat the other.

WHERE TO JUMP

Time: 10 to 15 minutes

Materials: Masking tape

Toddlers love to jump but usually need help finding out where to do it safely. This activity challenges your child to think before moving. Tape down a square on the floor and encourage jumping just inside of it.

Extensions:

- Tape down two lines that are 10 to 12 feet apart and challenge your toddler to run back and forth, putting both feet on a line before returning to the other.
- Tape a small square and have your toddler jump inside and outside of it.
- Let your toddler show you where to put 2 pieces of tape for both of you to run between.
- Have your toddler stand inside a larger square and jump up and down with you.

Apple Colors

Time: 5 to 10 minutes

Materials: Bowl or basket of yellow, green, and red apples ($), pieces of yellow, green, and red paper ($)

Sorting is an early decision game that makes young children feel competent and successful. Place the pieces of colored paper in front of your child and work together to sort the apples onto the papers according to their colors.

Extensions:

- Cut the apples into bite-sized slices and sort them again, talking about the task as it is done and nibbling along the way.
- Taste each kind of apple and decide on favorites.
- Have your child taste the apples with eyes closed to see if the different apples taste the same.
- Ask your child which apple is the prettiest and share your own preference.

Bedtime Magic

Time: 15 minutes

Materials: None

Young children often resist bedtime, but by designing a transition together that is regular and predictable, a great deal of conflict can be avoided. Write down the order so you can refer to it later. For example, you might decide to sing a particular song, rub the tummy, and then rock in a rocking chair. Keep the same order and approximate amount of time until the routine becomes a habit. Children can develop the necessary coping abilities to manage bedtime if you have faith in them and give them a chance to work past the emotional reactions and crying.

Extensions:

- If there is a fuss, tell your child that one part of the routine can be changed, but that everything else must stay the same.
- Draw pictures of the routine and hang it where your child can review it and learn the sequence.

Choice Tickets

Time: 5 to 10 minutes

Materials: Paper, scissors

Cut the paper into ticket-sized squares. Whatever the behavior difficulty your child is having, such as staying in bed at night, give her a ticket or 2 that can be used to choose an alternative. For example, at bedtime, your child might spend one ticket to come back for another hug and another to get a drink.

Extensions:

- Determine a reward if your child saves the tickets and accumulates a certain number.
- Let your child reward you with tickets that you can redeem for hugs and kisses.

Choose an Activity

Time: 20 to 30 minutes

Materials: Light cardboard or heavy paper, glue or tape, magazine pictures, felt pens ($)

Talk about things that your child likes to do at home, and use squares cut from the cardboard or paper to draw a picture of each activity, or look for pictures in magazines to glue or tape on. Store in a place where your child can look at them to choose an activity that you can do together. This way, the next time your child is bored, you can use his own choices to get him involved again.

Extensions:

- Make a set of play activity cards for when you are traveling or waiting in a restaurant.
- Make a set of weekend cards that are geared to fun with the whole family.

Color Sorting

Time: 10 to 15 minutes

Materials: Several small plastic bowls, small colored objects, or colored table blocks ($)

Learning to sort colors takes time, but this is a good way to begin practicing decision making. Put the plastic bowls on the table and assist with sorting a few of the colored objects by size or color into the bowls.

Extensions:

- Talk about the colors as you sort, using their names.
- Work together to sort all of one color for you, and all of another color for your child.
- Turn the bowls upside down and ask your child which color is under each.

Dinner Dishes

Time: 5 to 10 minutes

Materials: Mealtime utensils

Sometimes decisions are tied to particular tasks and skills. Ask your child to help you set the table by counting out the right number of utensils for everyone in the family and putting the utensils on the table.

Extensions:

- Count out the right number of napkins and ask your child to put them by each plate.
- Let your child decide which food should be passed around the table first.

Earned Rewards

Time: 5 to 10 minutes

Materials: Heavy cardboard, pencil

It can be difficult to get young children to comply with bedtime routines, tooth brushing, etc. To put the decision on your child, offer a reward card numbered from 1 through 10. Cross out a number each time your child complies with your directions. Completing the card earns a predetermined reward, such as dinner out at a favorite restaurant or a trip to the park.

Extensions:

- Let your child think of other rewards.
- Keep a card on hand for good behavior waiting in lines or in traffic.
- Let your child cross off numbers on a coupon made for you when you are good.

Edible Art

Time: 15 to 30 minutes

Materials: Large plate; pieces of healthy foods like broccoli, shredded lettuce, carrot rounds, celery sticks, orange slices, raisins, applesauce, etc.

Let the plates be faces and decide how to create your own edible people using the ingredients that are laid out.

Extensions:

- See if your child would like to trade individual pieces by eating one off the face to get a new one.
- Talk about which foods you like and ask your child to create a custom face for you from your choices.

Empty Space

Time: 10 to 15 minutes

Materials: Paper, scissors, crayons or felt pens ($)

Creativity and decision making come naturally with this challenging activity. Cut a hole out of each piece of paper and use the paper to color on. Do not give any directions about how to use the empty space. Many children will use the hole to create a picture or will place their marks purposefully around it.

Extensions:

- Demonstrate using the hole in a picture by making it into something specific, such as an eye or a bagel hole.
- Give your child another paper with the hole in a different place or of a different size.
- Practice tearing holes in paper before coloring.
- Use one of the holes to peek at each other.
- Search together for things that have holes.

Favorite Things

Time: 10 to 15 minutes

Materials: None

By age three, your child is forming opinions about likes and dislikes and will enjoy sharing them. Sit down in a quiet spot and ask your child questions about your favorite shirts, food, animals, and other things. Share your own in response.

Extensions:

- Talk about things you buy at the grocery store, adding ways either of you might like to alter that list.
- Take turns showing each other some of your favorite belongings.

Garden Book

Time: 10 to 15 minutes

Materials: Paper for mounting photos, a camera ($)

You can expand your child's appreciation of your garden by taking individual photos together and displaying them on paper or an album. Next year, use the photos so your child can help to select which vegetables or flowers to plant together.

Extension:

- When you prepare a meal with something that was in the garden, have your child find the corresponding photo and display it on the dinner table.

I Dress Myself

Time: 5 to 10 minutes

Materials: None

Learning to put on clothing is a huge step forward in developing self-care skills and is one of the best ways to encourage decision making. The motor skills to dress easily are still emerging, and it will be some time yet before your child can dress without help. In the meantime, let your child take some control by deciding what to put on first or what color to wear.

Extensions:

- Let your child pick out and wear a favorite shirt.
- Ask your child how to decide which pants will go with which shirt.
- Ask about the different kinds of shoes and how to know which one to put on which foot.
- Challenge your child to work with buttons, snaps, zippers, and Velcro.
- Ask your child to ask for help only on those articles that are too difficult. Count how many there are and work to make the number smaller over time.

Jars and Lids

Time: 15 to 30 minutes

Materials: Assorted jars with matching lids

This activity is not as easy as it might seem and can require many trial and error attempts until the correct decision is reached. Collect glass jars and their lids and mix them together in a box. Encourage your child to match them up, screwing the lids on the matching jars. When finished, remove the lids and mix them back together in the box.

Extensions:

- Color code the jars and lids for an easier version of the game.
- Have your child take away a lid and begin again. There should be a jar left without a top when finished.
- Play the game by beginning with the largest caps or jars and working toward the smallest.

Magnet Play

Time: 10 to 15 minutes

Materials: Refrigerator surface, numeral, alphabet, or other decorative magnets ($)

This is a quiet activity that can keep fingers busy while you are preparing dinner. Keep a container on hand that is filled with hand-sized magnets and let your child arrange them on the refrigerator while you talk to each other about the task.

Extensions:

- Challenge your child to place the magnets purposely; for example, all on the bottom, way up high, etc.
- Take the magnets around the house and see where else they will stick.
- Make up a story that incorporates the magnets while you are working, directing your child to move them and arrange the story.

Pet Store

Time: 30 minutes

Materials: Neighborhood pet store

Children love to see animals, and a pet store is a good place to safely explore them while practicing observing and choosing. As you visit, challenge your child to pick her favorite. (Agree ahead of time that this trip is for looking only.)

Extensions:

- Pick the cutest, funniest, or laziest.
- Talk about what each animal eats.
- Visit a bookstore or library and look for pictures of baby animals, talking about what makes baby animals different from full-grown ones.

Big to Small

Time: 5 to 10 minutes

Materials: Cardboard dowels made from empty paper-towel rolls, scissors

Visual discrimination and decisions are required in this activity. Cut the dowels into pieces of differing lengths and work together to arrange them from smallest to biggest or from biggest to smallest.

Extensions:

- Have your child hold 2 pieces and decide which is smallest or largest using his sense of touch, with his eyes closed.
- Lay the dowels flat in a line across the table according to size.

Color Lotto

Time: 10 to 20 minutes

Materials: Paint-chip samples from a paint store (2 of each color)

This is a nice quiet activity that you can do together. Cut the samples into single pieces, 2 of each, and mix them together. Because the colors are very close, this game takes attention to detail as the child decides which color chips are the same and pairs them up until all are matched.

Extensions:

- Remove one chip and repeat the game until the lone member is left.
- Have your child sort the colors into 2 piles: likes and dislikes.
- Sort into piles of similar, but not identical, colors such as pinks or greens.

Consequences

Time: 5 to 10 minutes

Materials: Plastic containers, paint ($), clay or play dough ($)

Children can be lazy about putting craft materials away. You can help to drive home the importance of deciding to clean up properly by setting up an experiment with small amounts of different kinds of paints, clays, or play dough. Put some into containers with lids and leave some out. Leave overnight and check together to see what happens to the materials the next day.

Extension:

- Help your child try to reconstitute the dried-out material with warm water to see if it can be salvaged.

Counting Clips

Time: 15 to 20 minutes

Materials: Pencil, a box of large paper clips, package of 3 x 5–inch index cards ($)

This is a fun way to learn about numbers while making discriminating choices. Write the numerals 1 through 10 on individual 3 x 5–inch cards and assist your child with deciding how many paper clips should be attached to each card to correspond to that numeral.

Extensions:

- Draw the corresponding number of dots under the numeral on each card.
- Have your child pick the card that represents his age.
- Place a miniature marshmallow ($) on each dot and eat them as they are counted.

Dawdling Dresser

Time: 10 to 15 minutes

Materials: Clothes

Dressing can be one of the most challenging areas for young children when it comes to self-control. Try telling the dawdler to pick a color and give directions accordingly. For example, say, "You can put on anything that goes on the legs and feet and I will do the rest."

Extensions:

- Think up ways to dress together, such as alternating the selection of clothing to put on, so there is a sense of accomplishment when finished.
- Pick a day (when you aren't going anywhere important) and agree that you will pick your child's clothes and they can pick yours.
- Rotate clothes to limit choices and make it easier to decide.
- Dress together, talking about your choices.

Explore the Zoo

Time: Up to several hours

Materials: Small tablet, pencil, admission to the zoo ($)

Take a trip to the zoo together, armed with a small tablet and pencil for taking notes. Before going, decide on categories to hunt for, such as scariest animal, cutest, laziest, etc.

Extension:

- Review the results with the whole family at dinner that night talking about differences in opinions.
- Count how many different kinds of a certain animal there are, such as monkeys, elephants, or birds.

How Heavy?

Time: 15 minutes

Materials: Paper lunch bags, items to put into them, stapler or tape

This is a decision-based task that will require real concentration. Put various items into the bags to weigh them down. Staple or tape them shut and challenge your child to arrange them from lightest to heaviest.

Extension:

- Challenge your child to make new weighted bags for you to sort. See if you agree on the answers.

In Charge at the Mall

Time: 30 minutes to 1 hour

Materials: None

Take a trip to the mall and plan together ahead of time, writing down the itinerary you will take. Make it clear beforehand which purchases are allowable and which are not. Help your child to think about a variety of things to see including elevators, escalators, pet store, colognes, shoes, etc.

Extensions:

- When you get home, talk about the trip and ask what could have been done differently.
- Draw a map of the mall, marking highlights that you visited.

Keys and Locks

Time: 20 to 30 minutes

Materials: Shoe box, assorted keys and padlocks ($)

Young children love the challenge of handling adult objects and will spend a lengthy period trying to determine which key goes to which lock, a decision that will be largely trial and error. Separate the keys from their locks and mix them together in a shoe box, challenging your child to match them up by trying them out.

Extensions:

- Add an extra key, letting your child know beforehand.
- Ask your child which lock is the easiest to open and which is the most difficult.
- Let your child offer the game to another adult and supervise his attempts.

Measure Up

Time: 15 to 30 minutes

Materials: Old, broken pieces of crayon

You can create a game using old crayons by challenging your child to spread the pieces out and sort them into piles by color.

Extensions:

- Have your child begin again and sort the pieces into small, medium, and large piles.
- Have your child find the biggest and the smallest single crayons.
- Draw the length of the smallest piece that should be saved and have your child use it to measure and discard those that are too small.

New Tastes

Time: 5 to 10 minutes

Materials: Food toppings like grated cheese, yogurt, raisins, popcorn, salsa, or guacamole

Try broadening your finicky child's menu while aiding good choices by offering familiar toppings to new or less desirable foods. For example, your child might choose to sprinkle popcorn onto vegetable or pea soup or coconut onto squash.

Extensions:

- Let your child go through the refrigerator to find favorite toppings, being careful to remain nonjudgmental about any unusual combinations.
- Let your child help with a shopping list of suitable toppings and some healthy (and maybe not so favorite) foods they can be served on. Remind your child that a topping can only be chosen if it goes on a healthy food.
- Ask your child to make a simple snack for you, based on things that you like.

Pick a Blossom

Time: 10 to 15 minutes

Materials: Local florist shop

A fun outing could include a stop at a florist shop to walk around slowly looking at all the flowers to decide on the prettiest.

Extensions:

- Ask your child to decide which 3 flowers would go well together in a bouquet.
- Ask your child to pick a flower that they would not choose and ask why.
- Visit a nursery and pick a packet of flower seeds ($) to plant together.
- Ask the salesperson which flowers are available for purchase as a single blossom ($) and let your child select one to take home.

Shell and Pea Game

Time: 5 to 10 minutes

Materials: 3 small plastic cups, small object

Place the 3 cups open-side down on a table. Let your child watch you put the small object under one cup and then rearrange the cups as he watches. Ask your child to decide where it is.

Extensions:

- Let your child take a turn at mixing while you do the guessing.
- Use 2 small objects and ask your child to pick the cup that has nothing under it.

Size Them Up

Time: 5 to 10 minutes

Materials: Small empty boxes wrapped in newspaper, extra newspaper

Put varying amounts of folded and densely packed newspaper inside the boxes and then wrap the boxes in newspaper so they look similar. Challenge your child to sort them from lightest to heaviest.

Extensions:

- Arrange the boxes from largest to smallest, helping your child to focus on size instead of weight.
- Fill the boxes with favorite toys and let your child open them as presents.
- Talk about a big gift for a big person and a small gift for a small person.
- Give the little box to a doll or stuffed animal and the big one to another family member.

Smile If You Like It

Time: 15 minutes

Materials: Paper, cup with a 3-inch diameter, pencil

A fun way to get your child to decide to try new foods is to give them control. Cut the paper into 3 circles 3 inches wide by tracing around a cup. Let your child draw a face on each of the three circles. One face should be smiling (I like it!), one sad (No, thanks!) and one should have a straight line for the mouth (I don't care.) Let your child use these faces to express opinions about new foods tried.

Extensions:

- If you wish, you can put a small magnet on the back of each circle and keep them handy on the refrigerator.
- Use the faces to get your child's opinion on other decisions made during the day.
- To resolve conflicts, pick a face that represents how you feel about your child's behavior and share it with her. Talk about ways to change the situation and get to another face.

Sorting Laundry

Time: 15 to 30 minutes

Materials: Laundry that has just been taken out of the dryer, laundry basket

The mix of newly washed laundry can let your child practice sorting and decision making. Work together to sort the clothing by person and then fold and deliver it to its correct place.

Extensions:

- The task could include sorting the clothes by the room where they belong and then delivering the folded clothes to their proper place.
- Sort the clothes by types, such as socks, dishtowels, etc.
- Teach your child to presort the laundry by lights and darks and help you put it in the machine with measured detergent.

SORTING GAMES

Time: 15 to 30 minutes

Materials: Empty egg cartons, marbles, or buttons to sort ($)

Deciding which goes where makes this game interesting to the young mind. Challenge your child to sort a collection of marbles or buttons by colors into the egg carton sections. This is also an excellent school-readiness skill.

Extensions:

- As a special treat, sort brightly colored candies that are mixed together.
- Add small cereal pieces to sort by color or shape.
- Have your child put a specific number of pieces in each carton section.

THINGS THAT ARE ALIKE

Time: 15 minutes

Materials: Common items such as silverware, food cans, socks and shoes, nails, keys

Grouping items used in everyday life is an important decision-making task that you can help to emphasize as you do chores around the house. With your child working next to you, gather items that are out of place in a room and return them where they belong.

Extensions:

- Challenge your child to put the silverware away from the dishwasher.
- Ask your child to put the shoes in the closet into matched pairs.
- Let your child group nails or screws of different sizes into jars or other containers.
- Ask your child to rearrange a cupboard of canned goods by sizes or by category (fruits, vegetables).

3-D Collage

Time: 20 to 30 minutes

Materials: Shoe-box lid, glue, 3-dimensional objects such as empty thread spools, film containers, marbles, old costume jewelry, yarn or string, button, etc.

Spread the objects to be glued out on a table and talk about how you might use them to create designs. Work independently to arrange them on the box lids. Ask questions of each other regarding possible arrangements as you go along, before they are actually glued down.

Extensions:

- Consider stacking items vertically as well as horizontally.
- Draw a simple pattern (circle, triangle, etc.) on the lid and incorporate it into the placement of items.
- Spray paint ($) and sprinkle with glitter ($).

Budgeting 101

Time: 5 to 10 minutes

Materials: Weekly allowance ($)

Learning to budget and save can become a habit if it is learned early. Involve your child in working out a plan to put certain percentages of the weekly allowance into categories like savings, charity, college fund, car fund, spending, etc.

Extensions:

- Set savings goals and decide on rewards as goals are reached.
- Review the financial goals that each of you have set at regular intervals to check progress and to make necessary adjustments.

Buying Power

Time: 5 to 10 minutes

Materials: None

Avoiding impulse buying can be learned from the habit of delaying a purchase when it is not planned. Before a purchase is made, take time out to work together to find 3 prices for the item, and agree to wait 2 weeks to decide if the purchase is still desired.

Extension:

- Keep track of and talk about the results and what is learned.

Cityscape

Time: 45 to 60 minutes

Materials: Small boxes, glue, large piece of cardboard cut from a brown packing box (at least 18 inches square), paint ($), small paintbrushes ($)

Creating artwork always involves decisions and this project offers many such possibilities. Work together to paint the boxes and when they have dried, glue them onto a large piece of cardboard to create a city.

Extensions:

- Challenge your child to think of other things that could be added, such as small cars to drive through the streets, grass and trees to make parks and yards, etc.
- Make city and street signs. Include things like elevation and population.

Coin Game

Time: 15 to 30 minutes

Materials: 18 coins, paper, pencil

This is a mentally challenging math game with consequences for each decision. Lay 18 coins on a table and tell your child to remove 1, 2, or 3 coins at a time. Take turns picking up coins. Whoever picks up the last coin is the winner. Use paper and pencil to tally scores, if desired.

Extensions:

- After playing several games, talk about what happened and how to strategize to win.
- Keep track of wins and chart results over a period of several days to see if there is improvement.

Earn Your Way

Time: 10 to 30 minutes

Materials: Paper, pencil

With this activity you work together to think of ways to earn money. Brainstorm a list of possible household chores and attach a payment value to each. Let your child select which chores and how many to do to earn her pay, including an option to do nothing and earn nothing.

Extensions:

- Think of new tasks that can be added and let your child suggest payments.
- Make a list of the things you do to earn money and share it (but not your salary) with your child.

Family Movie Time

Time: 1 to 2 hours

Materials: Pencil, movie video ($), healthy snack

Work together to plan a movie night for the family. Include interviews of all participants to pick a movie and menu that will work for everyone.

Extensions:

- Make flyers with details of the upcoming event to give to family members ahead of time.
- Repeat this interview process to plan a family outing.
- Work together to plan a short family vacation, including sending for brochures or researching on the internet.

Favorite Foods

Time: 20 to 30 minutes

Materials: Paper, pencil

Divide the paper into 2 columns, labeled *Foods I Like* and *Foods I Do Not Like*. Work together to think of all the foods that fall into those 2 categories and create separate lists to share.

Extensions:

- Talk about nutrition and how each of your choices could be altered.
- Make up a list of foods on the *Do Not Like* list that could be tried and perhaps moved to the other list. You may want to consider a reward, such as being able to pick a helping of a food they do like for each one moved over.
- Take your child shopping to purchase, prepare, and eat 2 foods on the *Like* list and 1 on the *Do Not Like* list.
- Brainstorm different ways to prepare foods on the *Do Not Like* list to make them acceptable and experiment with them.

Fun Money

Time: 10 to 15 minutes

Materials: Newspapers or magazines with grocery coupons

Work together to go through the newspaper and cut out coupons for things you need to buy, talking about not buying unplanned items just because there is a coupon.

Extensions:

- When you have finished shopping, give your child the money saved with the coupons.
- Select a local charity together and donate the money saved, in person if possible.

Garden Plan

Time: 1 to 2 hours, plus maintenance

Materials: Gardening tools, paper, pencil, packaged seeds ($)

Let your child select a designated number of seed packets after you have sketched out a rough layout of the garden together. Check the packet for growing information before making a final selection. Plant each seed packet as directed, mounting the seed packets on sticks in each garden area so you can both identify and compare seedlings as they sprout.

Extensions:

- Have your child chart which plants are easier to grow.
- Have your child sketch out a garden for next year based on what has been learned.

Hang It

Time: 15 to 20 minutes

Materials: Picture that needs hanging, hammer, nail, measuring tape

Decide where you want to hang a small picture and give your child directions such as, "Hang the picture six inches above the bookshelf." Help to plan the steps needed to make this task successful.

Extensions:

- Talk about ways to improve the process.
- Work together to plan an arrangement of 2 to 4 clustered pictures.

Matched Sets

Time: 10 to 15 minutes

Materials: Tall jar or basket, hand saw, wooden dowels ($)

Cut the dowels into matched pieces of varying lengths. Put them into a basket and play a game of matching them into pairs, using only touch.

Extensions:

- Repeat using the eyes and talk about the difference in the process.
- Take 1 away and match pairs without looking so that there is 1 left over.

No Way

Time: 10 to 15 minutes

Materials: None

In this game you take turns deciding how a story should develop. Begin with a simple sentence and have your child say, "no," and then change a word. Next, you say, "no," and change another word. Continue until you both agree to start over again with a new sentence.

Extension:

- Set a time limit on the game and see how silly you can make the sentence within that time frame.

Official Tallies

Time: 10 to 30 minutes

Materials: Paper, pencil, clipboard ($)

Clipboards are grown-up tools that children love to use. Work together to think of a place in the house where a common family activity could be tallied, such as when lights are turned off, when someone cleans up the bathroom, etc.

Extensions:

- Share results with the family and agree to implement any needed changes.
- Get several clipboards so you can do several surveys at the same time.
- Keep a clipboard in the car for noting ideas and conversations that you think of when you are traveling together.

Organize It

Time: 15 to 20 minutes

Materials: None

Pick an area such as a drawer or closet that belongs to your child. Talk about how it might be better organized and make decisions about various alternatives for improving its usefulness. Then, clean and rearrange it together. Several days later, discuss the decisions made to determine additional changes.

Extension:

- Let your child organize a drawer that belongs to you, asking the necessary questions to carry out the task.

Pick a Snack

Time: 5 to 10 minutes

Materials: Food storage containers, healthy snacks

Keep the containers filled with healthy snacks so there is always a good eating choice available without asking. Suggestions could include raisins, baby carrots, bell pepper strips, zucchini rounds, dry roasted peanuts or sunflower seeds, or carob chips.

Extensions:

- Let your child help to prepare the snacks in the containers.
- Make a shopping list of healthy ingredients for your next shopping trip together.

Quick Change

Time: 15 to 20 minutes

Materials: None

Face each other and take a good look at the details of your clothes, hair, accessories, and so on. Turn your backs to each other and agree that one of you will make a change, such as removing a watch, unbuckling a buckle or untying a shoe. Turn back around when both of you are ready and try to identify the change.

Extensions:

- Increase the number of changes done during a turn.
- Provide a pile of extra clothing and articles to add on.
- Play the game by changing something in the room.

Shopping Spree

Time: 45 to 60 minutes

Materials: Paper, pencil

Use newspaper ads to come up with a grocery shopping list together. Check current supplies to see if any staple items need to be added to the list. The shopping excursion should include selecting items, checking for the correct change, packing the groceries to take home, and putting them away.

Extensions:

- Check each aisle carefully together to identify (but not necessarily buy) the food that is the strangest looking, the most colorful, or that has the weirdest name.
- Set a budget together and eliminate items if there is not enough money.
- Give your child a set amount to spend independently.

Squeegee Painting

Time: 15 to 20 minutes

Materials: White paper, a small window squeegee ($), paint or food coloring ($)

Cover the work area with newspaper and tape the white paper to the edge of the table. Drip colors along the edge and pull across with the squeegee.

Extensions:

- Experiment with quick and slow movements.
- Use wavy motions.
- Add a new color at the center of the page and pull it out from there.

Yarn and Glue Pictures

Time: 20 to 30 minutes

Materials: White glue, scissors, small bowls, dark paper, scraps of yarn ($)

Work together to cut the yarn into pieces of varying lengths. Dilute some white glue with water in a bowl and dip in each yarn piece, using the fingers to squeeze off the excess. Work independently to decide how to arrange them on paper and allow the work to dry for several hours when finished.

Extensions:

- Glue the pieces onto small boxes or clean small glass jars to make fancy containers.
- Use paper plates and make designs and faces with the yarn pieces.

kindness

Children learn kindness in much the same way that they can learn aggression—by example and by experience. You can model kindness for the children in your life through habits and lifestyle choices that are empathetic and generous. Children easily understand the idea of kindness, for we are wired to respond to triggers like sadness or distress. Even babies become agitated by the sound of a crying child.

Working to plant seeds of empathy and kindness takes time and countless repetition, for young children are naturally self-centered and egocentric, thinking primarily about their own immediate needs. It will be years before kindness is a well-anchored habit and choice. Getting along with family members and other children will be marked with the inevitable conflicts that we expect from young children, particularly as they struggle to share belongings and take turns. Nevertheless, it is never too early to begin teaching and modeling this valuable life skill, which is learned in bits and pieces.

As you work with your child to experience how acts of kindness feel, many joyful moments of understanding will occur, albeit for short periods of time. Your efforts are worthwhile, and the satisfaction felt when you praise a successful act of kindness will help to build an understanding of the acts of giving and receiving.

The activities in this chapter are designed to expose your child to opportunities involving kindness to others. They provide a beginning to a lifelong journey that can result in behaviors that allow your child to enjoy other people more fully and to thrive in many social settings.

Blow a Kiss

Time: 5 minutes

Materials: None

You can teach your baby to give a gift of love as you blow a kiss to her and encourage copying blowing a kiss by spreading open your arms and saying, "Blow me a kiss."

Extensions:

- Help your baby copy you and blow a kiss back.
- Blow kisses to each other in front of the mirror.

Feed Me

Time: 5 to 10 minutes

Materials: Finger food

When your baby is eating finger food, say, "Can I have some?" and guide a hand to your mouth. Eat in an exaggerated and playful manner as you enjoy the gesture of sharing.

Extensions:

- Take turns feeding each other.
- Pretend to feed toy animals or dolls.

Gentle Touch

Time: 5 to 10 minutes

Materials: None

Using special care handling babies sends strong messages of love and care. As you talk to your baby softly, you can pay special attention to the ways that you lift and move them to let them know how nice human contact can feel.

Extensions:

- Massage a body part gently, such as the arms or legs, and talk about what you are doing.
- Nuzzle your baby close to your face and whisper softly.
- Tell your baby what you are doing when you dress him or change his diapers.
- Respond to crying as soon as you can, showing that you understand the need for attention, whatever the reason.

Kiss It

Time: 5 to 10 minutes

Materials: None

Kindness goes a long way toward healing, so when the inevitable bumps and falls happen, hug your baby and say, "Kiss it." When you kiss the hurt, say, "All better."

Extensions:

- When you hurt yourself, ask your baby to kiss your hurt.
- Pretend that your baby's toy animals or dolls get hurt and take turns kissing and making them better.

Nose Rubs

Time: 5 minutes

Materials: None

How good it feels to get up close and personal. Face your baby and gently bump noses as you say, "I've got your nose."

Extensions:

- Use different voices as you move in and rub noses.
- Say, "Touch my nose," as you move forward, letting your baby copy you.
- Whisper the directions and move very slowly toward your baby, bumping noses and following with a hug.
- Nuzzle noses with a favorite stuffed animal together.

Air Walk

Time: 5 minutes

Materials: Two adults

Early steps are even more fun when fun-loving adults lift the toddler into the air as they are walking. In no time, your toddler will be lifting and jumping to help you out.

Extensions:

- Walk backwards and do the same thing.
- Lift your toddler up and spin her around in the air every few steps.
- Have your toddler walk forward or backwards with his feet on top of yours.

Animal Dress-Up

Time: 15 to 20 minutes

Materials: Some of your toddler's clothes, large stuffed animals

To give dolls and stuffed animals a new look, dress them up in your toddler's clothes. Talk about how nice they look, and thank your toddler for helping out.

Extensions:

- Add sunglasses and jewelry.
- Add a favorite hat.
- Make the animal talk about what you are doing.
- Have the doll say, "Thank you," for the new look.

Brush My Hair

Time: 5 minutes

Materials: Hairbrush

Show your toddler how to brush your hair and express your enjoyment and appreciation with these early attempts to give you pleasure.

Extensions:

- Pull out a hand mirror and say, "See how pretty!"
- Add a short spray of cologne to each of your heads to make your hair smell nice.
- Go together in front of a mirror and admire the work.

Flower Power

Time: 10 to 15 minutes

Materials: Flower from a garden

Go outdoors with your toddler and select a single beautiful flower to take together to a friend or family member as a happy surprise.

Extension:

- Pick a flower and give it to your toddler. Put it in the bathroom or bedroom in a vase where it can be seen and enjoyed.
- Put flowers in your hair or attach them to your clothes with a piece of masking tape.

Fruity Treat

Time: 5 to 10 minutes

Materials: Fruit juice, small paper cups ($), popsicle sticks ($)

You can make and share a gift that is both tasty and healthy by pouring fruit juice into paper cups and inserting wooden sticks before freezing. Once it is frozen, remove the cup and enjoy.

Extensions:

- Add some fruit that has been slightly mashed before freezing.
- Add a drop of food coloring ($) before freezing and sharing.

Go Get It

Time: 10 to 20 minutes

Materials: Box, 8 to 10 common household items, shopping bag or low shelf

Lay out the items in a box, large bag, or low shelf and ask your toddler to go and get things for you, one thing at a time. Select items that are easy to find and reach. Always say "thank you" as your toddler brings them for you.

Extensions:

- Review what your toddler has done, saying, "You got me a...."
- Give directions to give specific items for other family members or friends.

Helping Out

Time: 10 to 15 minutes

Materials: Cleaning tools such as rags, brushes, or a regular broom and mop with the handles cut down, plastic bucket

Kindness often means helping others, so let your toddler work right next to you with cleaning rags or small-sized brooms. Toddlers can feel quite competent dusting and scrubbing small spaces and feeling that they are helpful.

Extensions:

- Go outdoors together to clean the car or a sliding glass window.
- Pull weeds together in the garden or from potted plants.

Kiss Me

Time: 5 minutes

Materials: Tube of lipstick, mirror

Doing this activity helps to reinforce affectionate behavior in a playful way. Apply a little lipstick to your mouths and take turns kissing the mirror, using your names as you point to the kiss marks.

Extensions:

- Kiss each other on the cheek, leaving marks.
- Kiss each other at the same time.
- Show your toddler all the kisses on the mirror or your face and say how much you love her.
- Make kisses on paper and give them away.

Pillow Talk

Time: 5 minutes

Materials: Pillow

Comfort at just the right times feels so good. When one of you is tired, snuggle on top of a pillow for a few moments to pause and relish some brief respite.

Extensions:

- Get 2 pillows and lie together for a while.
- Use the 2 pillows to rest head to head instead of next to each other and feel each other's faces with your fingers.

Take Turns

Time: 5 to 10 minutes

Materials: Household objects

It will be a long time before sharing comes natural, but you can begin rituals of kindness by asking your toddler for a toy and returning it promptly after hugging it, making a game of passing it back and forth.

Extension:

- Place 2 identical objects between you and say, “One for me and one for you.” Make a game of trading the objects back and forth.

Valentine Hunt

Time: 10 to 15 minutes

Materials: Scissors, red construction paper ($)

Place hearts cut out from construction paper around a room and let your toddler search and find them. Each heart found can be redeemed for a kiss.

Extensions:

- Let your toddler hide the valentines for you.
- Pass out the hearts to family and friends.
- Put the hearts in a basket so you can play the game again when your toddler needs hugs and kisses.
- Offer each heart back one at a time, asking your toddler to place it on the shelf, in the box, etc.

Attracting Butterflies

Time: 10 to 20 minutes

Materials: Garden spot that can be viewed from a window; seeds or plants that attract butterflies such as zinnias, marigolds, asters, hollyhocks, or other purple, yellow, and orange flowers ($)

You can attract butterflies into your yard by creating a garden spot that contains the kinds of plants that nourish and attract them. Plant the seeds/plants compactly. Butterflies especially like purple, yellow, and orange flowers and those with short petals or flat tops that are easy to land on. Sit back and enjoy the beauty from your window together with a nice cup of tea.

Extensions:

- Make a butterfly viewing zone with some soft pillows and quiet music.
- Buy a small pair of binoculars ($) for close-up butterfly watching.

Care for a Plant

Time: 5 to 10 minutes

Materials: Empty jar, toothpicks, water, an avocado seed ($)

Caring for a plant is a vivid way to teach responsibility for things we love. First, you can enjoy the avocado for lunch. Then, poke 3 or 4 toothpicks around the middle of the avocado seed to support it over a jar. Fill the jar with water that covers the bottom half of the seed. Place in a sunny windowsill and replenish water daily. The seed will sprout in several days and continue to vine out into a beautiful plant if it is cared for.

Extensions:

- Sprout several seeds and give them as beautiful, natural gifts.
- Make a daily watering chart and let your child check off each time that he cares for his plant.

Chef for a Day

Time: 15 to 20 minutes

Materials: Ingredients for a simple recipe

Pick a simple recipe for a meal and let your child help to prepare it, allowing your child to present the food to the family with great flourish. French toast, grilled cheese sandwiches, and refrigerator biscuits are good items to begin with.

Extensions:

- Help your child plan recipes for an entire day.
- Designate a regular weekday, marked on the calendar, for Kid's Cook Day.
- Talk about healthy food and work with your child to pick and prepare a recipe that is healthy and a gift to those you both love.

Dog Cookies

Time: 30 to 40 minutes

Materials: ½ cup cornmeal, 6 tablespoons oil, ⅔ cup broth, 2 cups whole wheat flour, rolling pin, cookie cutters (a bone shape would be nice) or a glass for circle cuts

Mix the dry ingredients and add the liquids, using the hands to mix well. Add a few more drops of broth at a time if the dough is too dry. Roll out ¼-inch thick on a lightly floured surface with a rolling pin and cut with cookie cutters or a glass. Bake at 350 degrees for 30 to 35 minutes or until lightly browned. Let the cookies cool thoroughly before packaging.

Extensions:

- You may want to have some oatmeal and raisin cookies on hand so your child gets a healthy treat too.
- Put the cookies into baggies and deliver to family and friends who have dogs.

Fancy Water

Time: 10 to 15 minutes

Materials: Flower petals, water, small jars

This gift is free and easy to make. Take a walk to collect flowers and remove the petals together. Mix with a little water and seal tightly into jars. Show your child how to rub some on the arms or pour into the bath to add a nice smell.

Extensions:

- Find a picture of the flower used in the mixture and glue it onto the jar.
- Help your child put the name of the person receiving it onto the jar.
- Decorate the jar with glitter ($) or stickers ($).

Feed the Birds

Time: 20 to 30 minutes plus viewing time

Materials: Pine cones, flour, a piece of string or a Christmas ornament hook, birdseed ($)

Giving the neighborhood birds a treat engenders a sense of kindness to other creatures. Begin by making a stiff paste of flour and water. Spread it on the pinecone with the fingers and then roll the pasted pinecone in birdseed. Attach a piece of yarn or a hook and hang from a tree or set on a windowsill so that you can both watch the birds enjoying their treat.

Extension:

- Put bird pinecones into large plastic baggies and give to family and friends to feed their birds.

Healthy Banana Pudding

Time: 10 to 15 minutes

Materials: 2 bananas, ½ cup applesauce, 2 teaspoons of peanut butter, ¼ cup orange juice, plastic picnic knife ($)

Cooking healthy is an important way to teach kindness to the self and others. Your child can cut the banana into slices with the plastic knife and put them with the other ingredients into a blender for you to process until smooth. Pour into 4 small serving bowls and let chill before sharing.

Messenger

Time: 15 to 20 minutes

Materials: Common household items

Besides engendering an attitude of kindness, this activity can help your child practice following directions and completing tasks. Ask your child to fetch and deliver items from around the house in a particular order. For example say, "Go and get the doll off the bed in the guestroom and take it to Grandpa. Have the doll give Grandpa a kiss."

Extensions:

- Work together on a list of nice things you could do for your child, and do one when it is not expected.
- Make a list of nice things your child could do for you and share the list.

New Friends

Time: 5 to 10 minutes

Materials: Playground

Kindness can mean reaching out to others, an act that can be difficult for shy children. You can help to remedy this by getting down on your child's level and talking to other children who are playing nearby. Coax your child to joining in by suggesting a simple activity like climbing up the play equipment or digging in the sand.

Extensions:

- Ask another child what his name is. Share yours and coax your child to reciprocate.
- When you pass children in the grocery store or mall, encourage your child to say hello or to wave.
- Wave hello to other young children that you pass while walking or driving together.

Neighborly Fun

Time: 5 to 10 minutes

Materials: Cookies or fruit

Someone new in the neighborhood gives you a chance to model kindness to your child. Package up some cookies or fruit attractively and walk together to give it as a gift of welcome.

Extension:

- Make a similar delivery to a senior living nearby or in a residential facility.

Soapy Giants

Time: 15 to 20 minutes

Materials: 1 cup liquid dish detergent, wire coat hangar, water, flat cake pan, duct tape, ½ cup corn syrup ($)

The sensitivity that it takes to create and enjoy a giant bubble encourages gentle and caring behavior. Add the syrup and detergent to one gallon of water and pour into a flat cake pan. Use a large wand by bending a coat hangar into any shape you want and taping over the sharp ends with duct tape. Let the fun begin!

Extensions:

- Vary the size of the bubble to smaller sizes by cutting a circle out of a Styrofoam plate or cup and using it for the bubble tool.
- Take turns dedicating each bubble to someone you love.
- Give each giant bubble a name of its own as soon as it is created.

Adopt a Tree

Time: 20 to 30 minutes

Materials: Tree, tape measurer, paper, pencil

Find a tree that you both think is special and adopt it. Explore it by touch. Measure its circumference. Research its variety and particular needs for optimal growth, and devote some regular time to caring for it.

Extensions:

- Select a name for your tree and make a small name plaque to post at its foot.
- Start a seasonal diary to record your visits and observations of seasonal changes that occur.
- Make it a point to hug your tree together each time you visit.
- Take pictures of your tree at various seasonal intervals

Alphabet Cookies

Time: 30 to 45 minutes

Materials: Rolling pin, alphabet cookie cutters ($), cookie dough ($)

Work together to help prepare some homemade or purchased cookie dough, rolling it thin so you can each cut out the letters from your names. Include the names or initials of friends and family members to give as gifts.

Extensions:

- Help your child think of words like *best*, *funniest*, *nicest*, etc. and deliver cookies beginning with those letters.
- Cut out your child's whole name with cookie letters and eat one letter each day.
- Frost and decorate the cookies for a more festive product.

Beauty Shop

Time: 20 to 30 minutes

Materials: Articles used to style hair, such as a hairbrush, hair clips, headbands, ribbons, and a hand mirror

Playing beauty shop is a great way to role-play taking care of others. Take turns being the customer and beautician and talk about what you want done and what you are doing as you go along.

Extensions:

- Take turns giving each other a real shampoo, complete with a scalp massage.
- Before you go out for a walk, get fancy by dressing each other's hair.

Change Places

Time: 10 to 15 minutes

Materials: None

Part of learning to be kind is to experience and empathize with others. One way to do this is to pretend to be each other and act out accordingly. For example, one of you is a tired mommy and the other is a hungry child. When you are finished, talk about what it felt like in your roles.

Extensions:

- Pretend that each of you are other family members and act out a possible situation.
- Pretend to be someone imaginary (princess, fireman, painter) in a possible situation and talk about what it felt like.
- Take turns being a king and giving commands. Discuss what it felt like to both give and receive commands.

Clean It Up

Time: 15 to 30 minutes

Materials: Mild detergent, bucket, some rags

Kindness can mean helping out with chores and maintaining family possessions so they can be enjoyed. Assemble cleaning tools and work together to clean patio furniture, windows, or some other item. Give directions, but allow for independent work and don't demand a perfect product from beginners.

Extensions:

- Work together to wash the car.
- Use spray bottles to clean mirrors.
- Bring out dirty toys and scrub them.
- Ask other family members what you can clean for them.

Cookie Surprise

Time: 10 to 15 minutes

Materials: Small boxes, tape, scissors, cookies or crackers, wrapping paper ($)

The gift of a cookie would be nice enough, but if you wrap it so it is a surprise, it's even more fun to receive. Put a cookie or two in a small box and wrap before delivery.

Extensions:

- Make a list of people you want to give cookies to before the wrapping begins.
- Surprise your child by wrapping a cookie and leaving it where she will find it later.
- Look for recipes of healthy cookies that contain cereals, nuts, and dried fruits.

Healthy Ice-Cream Sandwiches

Time: 10 to 15 minutes

Materials: A spoon, slightly softened frozen yogurt or low-fat ice cream ($), honey graham crackers ($), plastic sandwich bags ($)

Be ready to deliver these gifts to friends and family members on a hot day. The slightly softened texture of the ice cream is important. Spread about 2 tablespoons between 2 graham crackers, using the back of a spoon. Put each into an individual plastic baggie as they are assembled. Store in the freezer until eaten or delivered.

Extensions:

- Sprinkle with granola, coconut, or chopped nuts before putting on the top cracker.
- Use chocolate graham crackers.

You're Great!

Time: 5 to 10 minutes

Materials: None

Giving and receiving compliments can feel awkward without some experience and practice. Take turn using words that describe what is good about each of you, or talk about things you are good at.

Extension:

- Write down words about each other and hang them for all to see.

Medals of Honor

Time: 10 to 15 minutes

Materials: Metal can or jar tops, ribbon ($), glue or a glue gun ($), glitter ($)

A great way to celebrate accomplishments is to have customized medals on hand to award. For each medal cut a 2-foot length of ribbon and trim the edges nicely. Fold over and glue the can top to the middle of the ribbon. Make a design or award designation (1st Place, winner, name, etc.) with white glue on the other side of the lid and sprinkle with glitter. Let dry thoroughly and tie the ends together so the medal can be hung from a button on the shirt or attached with a safety pin.

Extension:

- Plan a ceremony together to award the medals and include family and friends.
- Have an award ceremony for dolls or favorite stuffed animals and make up award categories together.

My Neighborhood

Time: 30 to 40 minutes

Materials: Paper, pencil

Take a walk together and write down all of the things that you think makes your neighborhood a special place. Be sure to include people, pets, services, beautiful things, etc.

Extensions:

- Draw pictures together to illustrate what you saw.
- Think of things that would make your neighborhood even nicer.
- Draw improvements in a "wish picture."

PRETEND THAT...

Time: 10 to 20 minutes

Materials: None

Problem-solving is an excellent way to teach the experience of kindness to others. You can do this by posing hypothetical situations and thinking of alternatives for good endings. For example, you could say: "Let's pretend that I just got home from work, and while I was cooking dinner the phone rang. When I was talking, dinner burnt. What could happen next?" Or, "Let's pretend that we have been eating dinner, and there's only one piece of pizza left, and we both want it." Make sure that your solutions always improve the outcome for everyone involved.

Extensions:

- Ask your child to tell you about difficult situations they have faced and how they handled them. Could anything have been done differently?
- Create a problem-solving book together by writing down examples of good ways to handle difficult situations. You can refer to them later when similar situations arise.

READ ME A STORY

Time: 10 to 15 minutes

Materials: Storybook

Invite your child to select a favorite storybook to "read" to you. Go through each page together and listen to her version, which may be quite close to the actual words. Your attention and appreciation will make your child feel both competent and important.

Extension:

- Before turning a page, see if your child can remember what happens next.
- Go back through the book again and work together to make changes to the story so that it becomes a kinder story.

Set the Table

Time: 10 to 15 minutes

Materials: Eating utensils

Family mealtime can provide companionship and conversation as well as nutrition, and it provides the perfect setting to teach kindness as well as good manners. Helping to set the table can calm your child and provide a transition that prepares her for participating appropriately as part of the family.

Extensions:

- Make name place cards together and let your child place them for each person.
- Work together to color napkins so each person has a special piece of art to use at dinner.
- Change who sits at the head of the table each time, and let that person be the honored guest, perhaps with a crown.

Something for Everyone

Time: 5 to 10 minutes

Materials: Piece of fruit

Set a piece of fruit on the table and think of at least 3 ways to get it. (Examples: grab, ask to share, trade, find another.)

Extensions:

- Think of 3 things to say if someone gives it to you.
- Think of 3 ways to ask for it politely.

Wrapping Paper

Time: 20 to 30 minutes

Materials: Paper, sponges cut into shapes such as stars and hearts ($), poster paint ($)

Giving gifts to loved ones and friends helps children to feel generous and proud. When they make the wrapping paper it comes in, so much the better. Pour a small amount of each color of paint into a separate saucer. Spread out the paper and dip the sponge into the paint, making sure to cover the entire surface. Make prints on the paper and repeat as desired for a beautiful gift-wrap paper.

Extensions:

- Print with a potato that has been cut into a simple shape.
- Sprinkle lightly with glitter ($) while still wet.

10 Good Things

Time: 10 to 20 minutes

Materials: Paper, pencil

You can help your child to appreciate all the good things that happen each day with this activity. Make lists of 10 good things that happened to each of you today, beginning with when you first opened your eyes. Take turns sharing the lists.

Extensions:

- Expand the time period to the last week, month, or year.
- Expand the number to 20, 50, or 100.
- Share copies of your lists with family members and talk about the blessings in your lives.

Brooms, Brooms, Brooms

Time: 10 to 20 minutes

Materials: Various kinds and sizes of brooms, a dustpan

This is a clean-up activity that is both practical and interesting. Gather as many kinds of brooms as you can find, such as push brooms, kitchen brooms, whisk brooms, etc. Let your child choose an indoor or outdoor area to experiment together with the various cleaning tools, sharing your results and observations.

Extensions:

- Make a list of chores that work best when done with each broom.
- Compare the function of brooms and hairbrushes.

Bug Catcher

Time: 30 minutes to 1 hour

Materials: Round empty oatmeal box with its lid, masking tape, piece of string, small piece of screen ($)

Observing and then caring for little insects teaches kindness in handling nature's creatures. Cut a large window in the side of the oatmeal box. Cut a small piece of screen to fit inside, taping the edges carefully to cover sharp edges. Punch 2 holes in the sides to add the string for a carrying handle. Catch bugs to study, and release where you found them when you are finished.

Extension:

- Use a small magnifying glass for observing.

Designer Memo Pad

Time: 30 to 40 minutes

Materials: White paper the size of the desired finished pad, services of a commercial copy center ($), a fine tipped black pen ($)

Use the black pen to draw and decorate a sheet of paper (whatever size you want the pad to be) at the top and bottom. You can add headlines such as *Grocery List*, or *Things to Remember*. Take the art to a copy store to have the page reproduced on pads of tear-away paper.

Extension:

- Use colored markers to highlight the finished product with a few colorful strokes.

Doggie Greeting Card

Time: 20 to 30 minutes

Materials: Glue, scissors, markers or crayons, optional plastic "google" eyes ($), construction paper ($)

The dog lovers in your life will love receiving these enchanting cards. Begin with a square piece of construction paper. Fold into a triangle and then fold the 2 tips of the folded side in to make the dog's ears. Put a face on the dog and use the space under the ears to write a message to a dog lover. Add eyes, if desired.

Extension:

- Package several cards into plastic baggies and give to dog-lovers.

Doggie Shampoo

Time: 20 to 30 minutes

Materials: Dog, bath tools, and shampoo

Treat a dog to a nice shampoo to show your love for the dog and owner. Shampoo the dog outside or in a bathtub and rinse well, adding a few encouraging remarks and songs as you complete the task together.

Extensions:

- Make flyers to advertise your services around the neighborhood.
- Visit a pet store to see various bath aids that are available and decide which would be nice to buy and which could be replicated.

Earth Day Project

Time: 20 to 30 minutes

Materials: Common household objects

The fourth Saturday of each April is celebrated worldwide as Earth Day. In preparation for this day of ecological kindness, think of ways to do the following:

Reduce: Buy products that are not over-packaged in individual servings; check household water usage for things like brushing teeth or washing hands.

Recycle: Buy recycled-paper products; recycle newspapers; recycle containers to use for storage of leftovers instead of using foil or plastic wraps.

Donate: Collect and give away old clothing or toys to charities.

Extensions:

- Organize the family to celebrate Earth Day with a specific task.
- Organize a neighborhood activity with friends and plan several activities. Make and distribute informational programs ahead of time.

Easy Soap

Time: 30 minutes

Materials: Microwave oven, microwavable cups or paper cups (these will get hot), plastic spoons, knife, optional cookie or candy molds ($), transparent glycerin soap ($)

Soaps make wonderful gifts for friends and loved ones. Set out all of the ingredients and cut the bars of soap into about 3 or 4 pieces. Put pieces in a cup and melt in the microwave for about 10 to 15 seconds. If it does not melt and bubble, you do not have pure glycerin soap. Have an adult use a potholder to remove and stir to mix thoroughly, pouring it into the molds before it hardens. Let it cool and harden for about 5 minutes. Store in little gift bags to give as gifts.

Extensions:

- Add flower petals and a dash of perfume or other scents.
- For children, add small plastic flowers or bugs ($).

Edible Greeting Cards

Time: 20 to 30 minutes

Materials: Powdered sugar, milk, graham crackers ($), food coloring ($), candied sprinkles ($)

These cards offer double enjoyment, a visual treat and then a snack. Use a graham cracker for a card and prepare a glue of powdered sugar and milk, mixed until smooth. Frost the crackers with one color and let dry for 10 minutes. Glue on candies and sprinkles to make a design.

Extensions:

- Spread the cards out on a tray and offer them to family and friends, allowing them to choose their favorite.
- Make a cone from wax paper ($) and pipe on frosting in simple designs or names.

Healthy Corn Chips

Time: 20 to 25 minutes

Materials: ½ teaspoon salt, 1¾ cup boiling water, 1 teaspoon margarine, ½ cup cornmeal ($), cookie sheet

Corn chips are a favorite snack and even nicer when they are healthy. Combine the cornmeal and salt in a mixing bowl. Pour in 1 cup of the boiling water and the margarine and stir until well mixed. Add the remaining boiling water and continue stirring. Drop by spoonfuls (half-dollar sized) on a lightly greased cookie sheet and bake at 450 degrees for 12 to 15 minutes or until golden brown.

Extension:

- Serve with salsa ($) or a sprinkling of cheese.

How Many Times

Time: 5 to 10 minutes

Materials: None

This is a useful game for soothing hurt feelings. You begin by saying, "I love you," 2 times. Your child can raise your number by any amount, such as doubling it to 4 times. You might respond by tripling that to 12 and adding 1 for 13. Continue until the math gets too high to continue and then begin again.

Extensions:

- Say, "I love you all the way to (choose a city, like Boston)." Reply with something like, "I love you all the way to Boston and then New York." Continue the play until you cannot repeat the whole chain of places.
- Substitute favorite things, like, "I love you as much as 3 ice cream cones." The reply might be, "I love you as much as 3 ice cream cones and 4 licking puppies." Continue as above for as long as you can.

Indoor Container Gardening

Time: 30 to 40 minutes

Materials: Drill; dirt; small stones; unusual containers for indoor plants, such as driftwood, buckets, or old an wagon; plants or seeds ($)

Drill drainage holes if there aren't any and then place a few stones over the drainage holes before adding the dirt. Seed packets will tell you how much sun is needed for a particular plant. Choices like ivy thrive even where there is not much sun. Place garden containers in spots where you will pass by them often. Most plants do best when watered only as the soil begins to dry out.

Extensions:

- Plant herbs and use them for cooking.
- Make smaller pots and give them as gifts when they are ready.

Magazine Holder

Time: 20 to 30 minutes

Materials: Large, empty cereal box; scissors; white spray or poster paint ($); light and dark green poster paint ($); sponge ($); cotton-tipped swab ($)

Decorate your house with a thoughtful addition that reduces clutter. Cut the top off the cereal box, and halfway across the top of the box, make a cut down and over to the side at a 45 degree angle. Paint the box white and let dry. Cut the sponge into a leaf shape and dab into shallow containers of the dark green paint. Rinse and repeat with the light green paint. Use the Q-tip to paint vines with the darker green.

Extensions:

- Personalize by painting on a name.
- Make a holder for storing the day's newspaper.

Mosaic Work

Time: Several hours, over time

Materials: White paper, colored paper scraps, scissors, glue

A mosaic is a gift that takes time, which makes it all the more appreciated. You can create one together by alternately gluing down cut pieces of colored paper scraps, discussing arrangement possibilities as the design emerges.

Extension:

- Begin in a specific way, such as at the edges, the corners, or in the middle of the paper and talk about how that alters the process.

My Special Tree

Time: 20 to 30 minutes

Materials: Garden tools, a new tree sapling ($)

This is a nice project to do with a loved one, for it can be revisited and appreciated for years to come. Pick the planting site; perhaps somewhere visible from the house so your child can easily see the tree's growth. Dig the hole, adding nutrients if desired, and examine the root ball to make sure the hole is big enough. Pack the soil around the root ball, and you have a living monument.

Extensions:

- Check out a library book or search the internet for information about how trees clean the air we breathe.
- Learn about different kinds of trees and how they change with the seasons.

Personal Paper

Time: 30 to 40 minutes

Materials: Clean Styrofoam meat tray, ballpoint pen, empty paper towel roll, glue, piece of cardboard, ink stamping pad ($), tracing paper ($)

To personalize notes and papers you can make customized designer stamps. Mark your design on tracing paper and put the paper, printed side down, on a clean Styrofoam meat tray. Trace hard over the design with a ballpoint pen to leave an impression in the Styrofoam. Cut out the area around the ballpoint imprint on the Styrofoam to use as your stamp. Glue a piece of cardboard to the back cut the same size as the new stamp to make it stiff, and glue on a small piece of paper towel roll for a handle. Let it dry thoroughly and cover the stamp with ink from the pad to print on paper or note cards.

Extensions:

- Use the same technique to make your own holiday cards.
- Print place cards for dinner.

Pressing Flowers

Time: Several days, over time

Materials: Small flowers that have been collected on a nature walk, such as violets, buttercups, daisies, and pansies, paper towels, heavy book

Flower pressing is an old art that captivates children and produces wonderful gift items. Take a nature walk together and collect a good sampling of small flowers. Place the flowers between sheets of absorbent paper towels under a heavy book. Keep the book in place for 3 to 4 days or until the flowers are thoroughly dried.

Extensions:

- Dried flowers can be used for a variety of decorative projects, such as when making greeting cards, bookmarks, or place mats, or to create works of natural art such as flower and leaf collages.
- Seal flowers ($) between sheets of clear contact paper and make into bookmarks or wallhangings.

Teach Me

Time: 10 to 30 minutes

Materials: None

Sometimes being kind is as simple as asking for help. Children are used to being told what to do, so it is flattering when you ask for help or instruction. Think of something that your child can do competently and ask for help. Listen courteously and don't interrupt. Afterward, be sure to express your appreciation.

Extensions:

- Teach your child something you learned from a relative or other adult when you were a child.
- Pair your child up with a younger child so he can teach an activity that he can do well to someone around his age.

physical ability 10

Few childhood tasks affect self-esteem as directly as the development of strong physical abilities. Infants turn over, crawl, and pull themselves upright to the applause of their families. Preschoolers scramble up slides and look down excitedly for adult encouragement. School-age children believe that they can run faster, throw farther and stand taller than anyone in the world. When we teach children the skillful use of their bodies, we equip them to live healthy lives, mentally and physically.

The early years are the years when healthy habits are formed, habits that allow for maximum physical development and success with valuable self-care skills. Without direct adult intervention, children will move about, but with varying degrees of success, some never reaching their full physical potential.

Before the elementary school years, young children acquire basic movements like walking, running, hopping, jumping, balancing, and climbing. They do this through group play, active games, ball handling, nutrition education, and following simple rules. The activities in this chapter challenge these skill areas in order to promote healthy minds and bodies in a natural play setting. There is also an emphasis on the importance of eating well and acquiring self-care routines that contribute to strong feelings of competence.

Your encouragement and participation alongside your child are key to an understanding of the physical skills, mental attitudes, and good habits that can carry them successfully into the future.

Bath-Time Fun

Time: 5 to 10 minutes

Materials: Washcloth, bathtub

Learning about the body is the first step in learning to control it. Hold a washcloth in front of your baby's face and ask, "Where's (baby's name)?" Quickly remove the washcloth and exclaim excitedly, "There's (baby's name)!" Repeat as long as your baby is amused.

Extensions:

- Put the washcloth in front of your face and play the game in reverse.
- Repeat the game using a bath toy.
- Cover a body part and say, "Where's your...(tummy, foot, etc.)?"

Feel the Rhythm

Time: 5 to 10 minutes

Materials: Rocking chair, music

A rocking chair provides movement that is soothing and familiar. Put on some music (it doesn't matter what kind) and hold your baby close to your chest while you rock together to the rhythm. Exaggerate the variances in the tempo that you hear.

Extensions:

- If your baby is willing, bring her to a standing position in your lap and allow her to put some weight on her feet.
- Exaggerate the rocking movements to very slow music.

First Water Slide

Time: 15 to 20 minutes

Materials: Plastic tarp, old shower curtain, or heavy-duty plastic garbage bag; warm water

Babies love water, and this is an activity that encourages water play and a good workout on a warm day. On a level lawn area, spread out the plastic and wet it with an inch or 2 of warm water, or let the water warm in the sun before you begin your play. Place your baby in a tummy or sitting position with you right alongside to encourage the splashing and water fun.

Extensions:

- Show your baby how to pat and splash with the hands.
- Trickle or pat a little of the water on your baby's face.
- Provide a wash cloth for your baby to sop up the water and suck on.
- Add a few rubber toys ($) to splash with.

Floating Catch

Time: 5 to 10 minutes

Materials: Variety of lightweight scarves of different colors and patterns

As you sit on the floor together, throw a scarf into the air and catch it in your arms as it floats back down. Throw another scarf and tell your baby to hold out her arms so that it falls there. Continue playing with both of you catching scarves.

Extensions:

- Wad the scarves into balls and throw them playfully at your baby.
- Put one scarf over your head and another over your baby's.
- Put one scarf over your head and let your baby pull it off.
- Put on some jazzy music and keep the scarves moving.

Go for It

Time: 5 to 10 minutes

Materials: Bright object or small mirror

This activity provides motivation for stretching and reaching. Place a bright object or small mirror just out of reach, making sure that your baby is successful at grasping it.

Extensions:

- Get down on the floor and move 2 toys (1 in each of your hands) toward your baby, ending up with giggles as both toys converge.
- Remove a toy from your baby's hands, placing it within reach and helping her to succeed at getting it back.

It's Me

Time: 5 to 10 minutes

Materials: Small mirror

You can help your baby learn the parts of the face while exploring the joy of a smile. Place a mirror on the floor so that you can take turns looking down into it. Point to and name body parts on yourself, the baby, and in the mirror.

Extensions:

- Put the mirror slightly out of reach where your baby is able to scoot and discover it.
- Cover the mirror with a washcloth and pull it off so your baby can see it. Repeat, making it a game.
- Draw attention to your baby in the mirror by calling his name.
- Show your baby how to kiss the face in the mirror and then kiss him for real.
- Dance your baby in front of the mirror and help with a wave of hello.
- Make faces into the mirror by opening your mouth very wide and saying, "mouth."
- Put your baby on your lap and move his arms and legs playfully in front of the mirror.

Many Parts

Time: 5 to 10 minutes

Materials: Masking tape

This game can help your baby learn that we all have body parts and that they have names. Give your baby a single piece of tape at a time and direct her to put it on a certain body part.

Extensions:

- Have your baby put a piece of tape on your body parts as you call them out.
- Let your baby name a body part and put a piece of tape there.
- Bright stickers ($) of any kind can be used instead of masking tape to mark body parts.

Mirror Images

Time: 5 to 10 minutes

Materials: Mirror, several bright-colored objects

Mirrors can present many surprises when you use them as play tools. Sit down with your baby in front of a mirror and jiggle a brightly colored object, saying, "Where is the... (doll, teddy bear, ball, etc....)?" Let your baby look in the mirror to find it by drawing attention to it there and then in your hand, to continue the game.

Extensions:

- Put on your best falsetto voice and pretend that a doll or toy is talking in the mirror.
- Place your baby's hand on your mouth or nose and draw attention to the mirror while your baby feels your face.

On a Roll

Time: 5 to 10 minutes

Materials: Small baby blanket

Babies learn to roll over on their own and don't need to be taught, but you can help to strengthen the muscles involved by laying your baby on her side and providing support from behind with a rolled up blanket. Lie down adjacent to your baby and encourage reaching for you. Eventually, she will topple forward and be able to do so at will.

Extensions:

- When your baby can roll on her own, tempt repetitions with a favorite toy or by smiling and talking.
- As your baby rolls over, gently roll her back so the movement is repeated, making it a game and talking about what you are doing as you go back and forth.

Pile Them High

Time: 5 to 10 minutes

Materials: Flat empty boxes from shoes, cereal, etc.

Deciding where to place things makes this activity fun and is an early lesson in balancing. Show your baby how to stack the boxes and then hand them to him, one at a time, encouraging and assisting with the stacking.

Extensions:

- Pile the boxes up and knock them down, encouraging your baby do the same. Exclaim playfully and repeat.
- Pile the boxes up and top them with a favorite soft toy before tumbling them over.
- Put a box behind a chair, letting your baby see you place it there. It is likely that your baby will scoot over to retrieve it so you can continue the game.

Sing and Sway

Time: 5 to 10 minutes

Materials: Soothing music

This activity provides one of the earliest experiences in the joy of rhythmic body movement. While sitting in a comfortable chair, hold hands and support your baby's putting weight on the feet to stand upright on your lap. Sing to the music and sway with your baby, back and forth. Many babies will respond by rocking up and down with the whole torso.

Extensions:

- Hug your baby to your chest and sway to the music.
- Get down on the floor and help your baby stand up and sway.
- Play some bouncy, rhythmic music and dance around the room with your baby in your arms.

Slide for a Day

Time: 5 to 10 minutes

Materials: Couch, table leaf

Sliding is a fun activity that raises body awareness and balance. You can make a temporary baby-slide by leaning a table leaf up against your couch and easing your baby down its surface.

Extensions:

- Help the baby go down headfirst, holding onto his feet.
- Challenge your baby to climb up, starting from the bottom.
- Have your baby roll a small car or stuffed animal up and down the slide.

Touch and Tell

Time: 5 to 10 minutes

Materials: None

Touch is one way to help your baby open up to your early attempts to respond to the physical environment. Begin by gently moving the legs, rubbing and lightly tickling them as you talk. Stretch them gently and move them rhythmically.

Extensions:

- Take your baby's hands in yours and clap them together while singing a song.
- Repeat with the feet.
- Clap your baby's hands and then clap your hands, talking about what you are doing.
- Gently massage your baby's cheeks with a finger. Do the same on his forehead, eyelids, and chin, saying the name of each part as you do it.

Tugging Game

Time: 5 to 10 minutes

Materials: Large, empty thread spool; piece of elastic about a foot long ($)

What fun to discover and then flex a muscle. Thread the elastic through the spool and tie it securely. Hold the elastic and dangle the spool in front of your baby, encouraging grabbing movements. When your baby has a good grip on the spool, gently pull on the elastic to create some resistance on the spool, being careful not to let go. Praise your baby for pulling with her newly discovered might.

Extensions:

- Tie the elastic to your hand and let your baby pull you near.
- Loop the elastic gently around your baby's hands and let your baby feel as you pull in an outward movement.
- Dangle several toys from the elastic so there are more choices to grab for.

Tummy Time

Time: 5 to 10 minutes

Materials: None

Playing from the tummy position allows for a different view of the world. Although it is recommended that babies sleep on their backs as a precaution against SIDS (Sudden Infant Death Syndrome), your baby can still benefit from exercise in the tummy position while awake. Lay your baby on his tummy and get down on that level, making faces and noises to encourage raising his head, which strengthens the neck and upper body muscles.

Extensions:

- Lay out some brightly colored toys so your baby can see them from this position.
- Get your baby's attention with any object and move it back and forth slowly so it is tracked with the eyes.
- Roll your baby to his side and then gently back to the tummy, saying, "Wheeeeeeee."
- Stand directly over your baby at your full height, and then move slowly down to a squatting position so you are very close.

Wheelbarrow Fun

Time: 5 to 10 minutes

Materials: None

You can help your baby gain upper body strength by gently lifting the legs while she is in the tummy position, encouraging her to move forward with the hands, if interested. This should feel good and be quite enjoyable if the baby is physically ready and if you are careful not to overdo.

Extensions:

- Do this activity while moving toward a mirror that can be seen at that level.
- Scoot toward a pillow laid out on the floor and collapse onto it.
- Do this activity to retrieve a slow moving ball.

Beach-Blanket Fun

Time: 15 to 20 minutes

Materials: Large blanket or towel

Your toddler will enjoy feeling the pull of gravity from the middle of a large blanket that you drag slowly around the floor. Talk about what you are doing and how it feels as you go.

Extensions:

- Take this activity outdoors.
- Go fast and then slow, using those words to talk about what you are doing.
- Ask your toddler to tell you when to go fast and when to stop.
- As trust is built, and if your toddler seems ready, 2 adults can toss her gently into the air a few times.
- Put a favorite doll or stuffed animal in the blanket and give it a ride.

Body Parts

Time: 5 to 10

Materials: Nose tissues

There are so many body parts and so many new words to learn, but this activity makes it fun. As you call out body parts (ears, eyes, nose, knees, back, etc.), put the tissues on that spot on your toddler.

Extensions:

- Call out the names and have your toddler place the tissue on you.
- Let your toddler call out the parts to you and check if you put the object on the right place. You may want to make a few obvious mistakes.
- Use a stuffed animal or favorite doll to play the game, identifying their parts together.

Brush My Hair

Time: 5 to 10 minutes

Materials: Hairbrush

Self-care habits are closely related to physical awareness and control. You can use a hairbrush to initiate play by brushing your own hair and then asking your toddler to join you with a small brush.

Extensions:

- Take turns brushing each other's hair.
- Take turns brushing a doll's hair.
- Add hats, scarves, or other hair adornments.
- Give each other a warm, bubbly shampoo.

Dump and Fill

Time: 5 to 10 minutes

Materials: Large coffee can with a lid; hand-sized objects such as large wooden beads, coasters, clothespins, snap beads, jar lids, etc.

Self-esteem is enhanced by being able to predict what will happen to materials, since this understanding allows a greater sense of control. It takes hours of filling and dumping to learn concepts like size, volume, and weight so that they are familiar. A simple way to encourage this skill is to fill an empty coffee can with hand-sized objects and then empty them out. Encourage your toddler to copy you.

Extensions:

- Provide small items in a low kitchen cupboard to put into a paper grocery bag.
- Place your toddler on a low table with a plastic tub of water and a pouring cup.
- Put appropriate, safe items into a purse and open it before handing it to your toddler.

Easy Tug-of-War

Time: 5 to 10 minutes

Materials: Small, lightweight blanket

Besides helping the young toddler to understand his own strength, this activity requires his balance and attention. Each of you take one end of the blanket and pull in your direction on a soft, carpeted area. Challenge your toddler's maximum strength as you take turns tumbling down.

Extensions:

- Add another adult to help your toddler.
- Use a scarf for this game and pull your toddler into a hug.
- Place a pile of pillows in the middle and pull your toddler onto it.
- Use a stuffed animal and have a gentle tug-of-war with each of you pulling on an arm.

Go Between

Time: 5 to 10 minutes

Materials: Two adults

The only thing better than one loving adult is two, and even more so when they join into this game. Sit on the floor a few feet apart and send your toddler back and forth between you with gentle pushes forward, rewarding each crossing with hugs of approval and kisses.

Extensions:

- Pull your toddler on her tummy across the floor.
- Call your toddler's name each time you catch and embrace her.
- Pull your toddler across to you by the feet from a sitting position.

Hide and Follow

Time: 10 to 15 minutes

Materials: None

In this version of "Hide and Seek," when the child finds you, you run ahead to another spot and hide. Reverse roles when your child tires of chasing you.

Extensions:

- Run together while saying, "Follow me," until one of you squats, calling the game to a halt. Action resumes when the squatter gets up.
- Use a hat to designate the leader and take turns wearing it and leading the action.

I Clean My Face

Time: 5 minutes

Materials: Washrag, warm water, mirror

Instead of fighting with your toddler to clean his face after a meal, hand over a warm wet washrag in front of a low mirror to encourage good self-care skills. Heap on the praise for whatever level of success is achieved.

Extensions:

- Get a second rag and wash your face at the same time.
- Smear a doll's face with a little food and let your toddler clean it.

Jumping High

Time: 10 to 15 minutes

Materials: Soft object to grab, piece of string or yarn ($)

Suspend an object above your toddler from the string and encourage reaching. First attempts will usually be stretches on the tiptoes. Demonstrate how to leap with a springy motion out of bent knees and be sure to help your child succeed by lifting him, if necessary.

Extensions:

- Help your toddler to stretch to full extension and talk about the feeling.
- Challenge your toddler to jump for the object like a rabbit, putting his hands up for ears.

Kitchen Helper

Time: 5 to 10 minutes

Materials: Silverware

Real jobs are fun for toddlers, who like to help out and show how much they can do with their emerging physical control. An easy one is sorting 10 to 12 spoons and forks into the silverware drawer.

Extensions:

- Hand your toddler the dirty spoons to put into the sink or dishwasher.
- Help your toddler to sort big and little spoons or forks into separate piles.

Name Game

Time: 5 to 10 minutes

Materials: Basket of laundry to be folded

While you're folding the clothes, you can reinforce knowledge of the parts of the body. Ask your toddler to name as many articles as possible: shirt, T-shirt, pants, socks, etc., and where they go on the body.

Extensions:

- Help your toddler make piles of clothes for each person in the family.
- Help your toddler to put all of the socks into a pile and sort them by owner.
- Scoot the basket through the house like a train and deliver the clothes together, talking about what you are doing.

Pillow Pile

Time: 5 to 15 minutes

Materials: Pillows

This is another vigorous and safe activity that teaches toddlers about their bodies. It doesn't take much room and is perfect for a rainy day. Provide a pile of pillows on the floor and invite your toddler to jump and roll onto it, getting close to the floor to protect her in case of a miss.

Extensions:

- Add music to enhance the fun.
- Spread the pillows out and show your toddler how to roll across them.
- Cover your toddler with the pillows.
- Have your toddler cover you with them.

Puff Bag

Time: 15 to 20 minutes

Materials: Newspaper, large green trash bag

This activity can be done indoors or out and can provide a vigorous workout with your encouragement. Work together to crumple enough newspaper to fill the empty trash bag. This helps to strengthen the hand muscles. Close tightly, pushing out as much of the air as possible. Toss the bag back and forth. Dispose of this when you are finished as the bag can pose a safety hazard.

Extensions:

- Let your toddler punch the bag.
- Try rolling the bag across the ground.
- Try rolling the bag back and forth.

Pushing and Pulling

Time: 10 to 15 minutes

Materials: Cardboard box that can be pushed, heavy objects such as books to put inside

Fill the box with items that make it difficult but not impossible to push. Challenge your toddler to move the box without demonstrating or giving directions about how to do it.

Extensions:

- Put something heavy in the way and let your toddler figure out how to move it.
- Put folded laundry in the box and push it from room to room as you put the clothing away.
- Put pillows into the box and let your toddler sit on top while you push.
- A small wagon ($) can be substituted for the box.

Rhythm Shaker

Time: 10 to 15 minutes

Materials: Raw rice, music, a large metal spice shaker with a handle ($)

Rhythm comes naturally to toddlers and helps them learn that they can control the movements of the body. This is a safe and easy rhythm instrument for your toddler, and it is easy to hold onto. Pour some uncooked rice into the shaker and replace the lid tightly. Put on some music and show your toddler how to shake to the tempo of the music.

Extensions:

- Put beans or gravel in the shaker instead of rice and compare the new sound.
- Give your toddler a shaker for each hand.
- Put on music and march around the house, using the shakers to keep step.
- Cover the shaker with bright adhesive shelf paper ($).

Roll Away

Time: 5 to 10 minutes

Materials: Medium-sized plastic ball ($)

As one of the first introductions to ball play, roll a medium plastic ball and encourage your toddler to chase after it and bring it back to you.

Extensions:

- Catch your toddler and have him ball up into your arms.
- Let him roll or throw the ball while you run after it.
- Challenge your toddler to kick the ball to you.

Toddler Train

Time: 20 to 30 minutes

Materials: 2 medium-sized brown packing boxes (about 18 inches or less across), brightly colored thick yarn ($)

This activity helps toddlers learn about their body strength. Cut the flaps off 2 good-sized boxes, and be sure to remove any protruding staples. Pass a cord of sturdy yarn, about 12 to 15 inches long, through 2 holes at the end of one box. Link the second box to it using another piece of yarn. Your toddler will love to pull this mini-train around the house.

Extensions:

- Challenge your toddler to throw things into the train.
- Challenge your toddler to push the train from behind instead of pulling it.
- Put something heavy into the train so your toddler can experience resistance. Remove the items to show the difference in strength required.
- Repeat and talk about putting things in and taking them out, about it being too heavy or just right.

Walk-a-Lot

Time: 5 to 10 minutes

Materials: None

Knowledge of what the body can do begins with learning to move it in different ways, at different paces, and in ways that challenge emerging balance. Encourage your toddler to walk in different ways with you—with high marching steps, with big striding steps, etc.

Extensions:

- Follow any cues that your toddler gives for ways to play this game.
- Use music of varying tempos to play the game.
- Try the game in shoes and then barefoot and talk about the difference.

Washing Game

Time: 15 to 20 minutes

Materials: Bathtub, washcloth

Learning the names of body parts makes your toddler feel special. Make up a melody for a washing song in which you challenge your toddler (by name) to wash the face, tummy, feet, hands, etc.

Extensions:

- Place the wet washcloth on a body part as you say its name.
- Squirt water from a squeeze bottle on each body part as you say it.
- Use a bath toy to jump from part to part, saying the names.

What's in the Soup?

Time: 20 to 30 minutes

Materials: Soup broth, raw vegetables

Invent an easy and healthy soup to fuel your physical activity as you talk about eating good foods to grow strong. Empty the broth into a pan and add whatever raw vegetable you have, slicing it into small pieces. Frozen or canned vegetables can also be used. Let your toddler add the vegetables and stir before simmering for 10 to 15 minutes.

Extensions:

- Give the soup a whimsical name that fits your moods, such as muscle mix or carrot curl.
- Add a few pieces of shaped pasta, like wheels or bows, for the last 10 minutes of cooking.

Balloon Fun

Time: 5 to 10 minutes

Materials: Package of balloons ($)

This activity helps your child to explore force and motion. Inflate the balloons and tie them off with the string. Suspend them from the ceiling just low enough to be reached, and hit them gently with the palm of the hand.

Extensions:

- Try to move the balloons by blowing them.
- Hit the balloons using only the head.
- Put your hands behind your back and walk through the balloons, letting them brush your faces.

Batting Balls

Time: 5 to 10 minutes

Materials: Balloons ($)

It will be a long time before your child has sufficient strength and hand-eye coordination to hit a ball with a bat, but this is an activity that can lead the way to that skill. Inflate a few balloons to use as balls and sit a few feet away from each other, batting them with the hands as they move slowly by. Dispose of the balloons after you are finished, as they pose a choke hazard.

Extensions:

- Kick the balloons across the floor or into the next room.
- Bounce a balloon off your child's head with a springing forward motion as you do so
- Use an empty paper-towel roll to hit the balloons.

Center of the Universe

Time: 5 to 10 minutes

Materials: Several scarves

Children love to spin around until they become dizzy and fall down. It makes them the center of their world as everything spins around them. Hold scarves out at shoulder level as you both twirl. Besides providing a rush of floating color, the scarf will also keep the arms high and enhance balance.

Extensions:

- Put on fast music and then slow music to spin to.
- Sew a bell ($) on the end of the scarf.
- Hold a scarf in each hand.

Crazy Walk

Time: 5 to 10 minutes

Materials: None

Following directions helps your child master the mind and body. Walk slowly around the room using music to set the pace. Call out a movement such as forward, backward, sideways, little steps, giant steps, like a cat, like an elephant, etc., and respond as quickly as possible.

Extensions:

- Try music with a different tempo.
- Move from room to room.
- Let your child call out the directions.

Giant Blocks

Time: 30 to 40 minutes

Materials: Brown paper grocery bags, newspaper, masking tape

You can make giant building blocks that challenge motor skills by filling paper grocery bags with crumpled newspaper (about 14 sheets into each bag), folding the tops about 8 inches down, creasing, and sealing with masking tape. Make enough so that large structures can be built, repairing tears as they occur during play.

Extensions:

- Add some smaller bags for variety.
- Paint or color the bags before stuffing.
- Tape the bags together as you build with them.
- See how long of a line you can make by laying them end to end.
- See how many can be stacked without falling over.

Human Airplane

Time: 15 to 30 minutes

Materials: 22-inch strip of heavy paper, masking tape, 1 or 2 small pinwheels ($)

The faster your child runs, the faster the pinwheel will fly. Tape the paper strip around the head to fit like a headband and insert a pinwheel straight up on the side so it can catch the wind.

Extensions:

- Experiment with the sound as you move slower and faster.
- Add a bell ($) to the center of each pinwheel.
- Tape pinwheels to the backs of each hand and run with them.
- Run toward a mirror or window so you can see the wheels moving.

My Body Size

Time: 5 to 10 minutes

Materials: Paved outdoor surface, chalk ($)

It is difficult for young children to understand their body size in comparison to others. Have your child lie on a shady stretch of pavement and strike a pose, and then trace around the body with the chalk. Label it with your child's name.

Extensions:

- Repeat in a different pose.
- Trace just a hand or a foot
- Color in features, like a mouth and eyes.
- Draw in clothes and shoes.
- Trace the body outline on a full-view mirror using a felt pen ($).

Paint the House

Time: 20 to 30 minutes

Materials: Bucket filled with water, large paintbrush ($)

This is an excellent activity for a hot day, and it uses both large and small motor skills. Fill a bucket with water and give your child a big paintbrush to paint the house, porch, sidewalk, or driveway. Move your lawn chair nearby so you can talk about the task and join in occasionally.

Extensions:

- Using chalk ($), draw shapes on the pavement and challenge your child to fill them up on the inside only.
- Paint big water faces with smiles and watch them slowly melt away in the sun.

Pamper Day

Time: Several hours

Materials: Things you each love

You can focus on the body by planning a pamper day just for the two of you. Consider bubble baths, lunch outside, a special movie, rubbing each other with lotion, and anything else that makes you happy.

Extensions:

- Design a pamper day for someone else in the family.
- Make coupons for pamper treats and give them away.
- Design a pretend pamper day for a favorite doll or stuffed animal and carry it out together, complete with dialogue.

Popsicles

Time: 5 to 10 minutes

Materials: None

This activity encourages control of the muscles. While lying on your backs with the legs together and the arms straight at the sides, say, "Popsicle," which is the signal to stiffen. Test each other by trying to pull the legs apart while they are stiff and straight with resistance. Next say, "Popsicles, melt," which is the signal to become limp again so that the legs can be pulled apart easily.

Extensions:

- Take turns thinking of and pretending to be other things that melt in the hot sun (such as a fudge bar, ice, ice cream).
- Link arms together while lying down and be a pair of popsicles.

Race Me

Time: 5 to 10 minutes

Materials: None

Growing muscles make young children feel powerful, and this is the perfect age for racing you across the yard.

Extensions:

- Play a pretend game of "Magic Shoes" and race around together, pretending you are flying horses or rocket ships. Talk about where you are going and why.
- With shoes on, try racing across different kinds of surfaces such as sand; dirt; and hilly, uneven surfaces.
- Try running barefoot on a grassy area.
- Set up an indoor running course that is safe for a rainy day.

Run to the Ribbons

Time: 10 minutes

Materials: Brightly colored ribbon ($)

This activity provides visual cues that will get most children moving at top speed. Cut the ribbon in 2-foot lengths and tie it to trees, doors, a water hose, etc. At the word *go*, run from ribbon to ribbon, touching each one.

Extensions:

- Let your child suggest objects to tie the ribbons to.
- Let your child give the directions about which ribbon to run to first.
- Use different colors of ribbons and give sequenced running directions by color.

Smart-Snack Station

Time: 5 to 10 minutes

Materials: Variety of healthy snack foods: cheese cubes, banana wheels dipped in orange juice to keep from browning, lightly steamed broccoli pieces, cut-up-hard-boiled eggs, cooked pieces of pasta, raw cut-up vegetables

Young children can have an uneasy time sitting still for meals, which makes it difficult to ensure that they are getting enough of the right kinds of foods to fuel their physical and mental activities each day. To develop healthy eating habits and to keep children from getting overly hungry, keep a healthy-snack station nearby for grazing between meals.

Extensions:

- Add low-fat salad dressing, yogurt, cheese sauce, or cottage cheese for dipping.
- Make a shopping list of healthy snacks together.
- Store choices in plastic containers that have pictures of favorite cartoon characters taped on them.

Stepping Up

Time: 5 to 10 minutes

Materials: Stepping stool, plastic cup

Many tasks can be done independently by providing a step stool that makes your child taller. Put a plastic cup by the sink to get drinks, and put out a toothbrush and washcloth.

Extensions:

- Provide soap and a hand towel for washing up.
- Provide a sponge and show your child how to clean up around the sink area.
- Keep a hairbrush handy so your child can clean up after play or before dinner.

Through the Tunnel

Time: 10 to 15 minutes

Materials: A few chairs, 2 to 3 sheets

With this activity, your child will learn about the space around his body and how to control his limbs in an enclosed space. Cover chairs completely with sheets, making twists and turns that will build spatial awareness and require control of arm and leg muscles. Although you may be too big to join in this fun, go partway into the maze to demonstrate, or greet your youngster at the exit.

Extensions:

- Add pillows to crawl over on the way through the tunnel.
- Let your child scoot a favorite toy through the tunnel.
- Add heavier blankets in some parts to make it darker.
- Use a flashlight while going through the tunnel.
- Put a favorite toy at the end as a surprise.

Wet Footprints

Time: 10 to 20 minutes

Materials: Brown paper shopping bags, shallow pan of water

This is an easy outdoor activity that provides a fun way to learn about the feet and the length of stride. Cut the paper bags at the seam so that they can be spread out flat. Step into the water with bare feet and walk across the paper bag, leaving footprints. Watch as they evaporate and disappear.

Extensions:

- Do this activity on the pavement on a warm (but not too hot) day and compare the stride of walking to running.
- Repeat the activity making hand prints.
- Try to cover the entire page before the prints evaporate.
- Challenge your child to find other objects outside that they can use to make prints.

Artwork on Parade

Time: 20 to 30 minutes

Materials: Strip of 1-inch-wide wood ($), screwdriver, screws, can of spray paint (optional) ($), clothespins with springs ($)

It is exciting to build something that is useful, so if you are cramped for art display space, glue wooden clothespins with springs to a strip of wood. Drill a hole at each end to put a nail or screw through for mounting on the wall. Spray paint, if desired. You can hang artwork using the pin after it dries.

Extension:

- Hang several strips, one under another, to cover a larger space or a whole wall.

Broad Jump

Time: 10 to 20 minutes

Materials: Board or other object 6 to 12 inches wide to jump over

Place the obstacle on the ground and run several feet, jumping over it without stopping before becoming airborne. Pull with the arms to gain speed. Make sure there is a soft landing area.

Extensions:

- Try running at different speeds and compare the results.
- Increase the running distance.
- Increase the obstacle height.
- Vary your jumps. Do a wiggly jump or a graceful jump. What else can you think of?

Easy Superhero Costumes

Time: 20 to 30 minutes

Materials: Pillowcase or towel, aluminum pie tins, bulb baster, large safety pins, roll of aluminum foil

Use safety pins to attach a pillowcase or towel to your child's shirt for a cape. You can make headbands or wrist braces from aluminum foil and add a bulb baster for a laser gun and an aluminum pie tin for a shield.

Extension:

- Use iron-on letters ($) to add superhero names.

Footsies

Time: 15 to 20 minutes

Materials: Masking tape or chalk ($)

This is another easy balancing game that works well when you join in the fun. Take turns walking along a tape or chalk line 4 to 5 feet in length, with the bare toes pointed inward (pigeon-toed).

Extensions:

- Walk with your toes straight ahead.
- Walk on the outer border of your feet with your toes curled under.
- Walk crossing your feet over alternately.
- Walk backwards.
- Walk wearing shoes and talk about what it feels like and how it changes things.

Gravity Challenge

Time: 15 to 20 minutes

Materials: None

Balance is steadily emerging and can improve with practice. With this simple exercise, you are the catalyst through your simultaneous involvement. Work together as you close your eyes and stand on one foot and then on the other, alternating feet. See if you can invent ways to make it easier, such as holding the arms out to the sides.

Extensions:

- Slow music can relieve some of the tension that gets in the way of balancing successfully.
- Balance with the legs crossed and the eyes closed.
- Balance on tiptoes with and without the eyes closed.
- Balance on the right leg with the left leg extended slightly sideways.

High Water

Time: 15 to 30 minutes

Materials: Piece of rope at least 6 feet long ($)

This activity strengthens the muscles and focuses attention. Tie one end of the rope to a tree or chair and hold the free side about 2 feet off the ground. Challenge your child to go under the rope by crawling or scooting on the tummy. Lower the rope a few inches each turn and repeat as many times as possible.

Extension:

- Keep track of ways to go under the rope and talk about which ones work best.

Indoor Sandbox

Time: 30 to 40 minutes

Materials: Large plastic tub ¼ full of rice, oatmeal, or cornmeal; drop cloth; kitchen utensils, jar

Because of the small play area used in this activity, the focus is on control of fine motor movements, particularly of the fingers and hands. Put the rice, cornmeal, or oatmeal into a large tub and place it on a canvas or plastic drop cloth to make cleanup easy. Add kitchen utensils for digging, spreading, and mixing. When finished, transfer contents into a jar with a tight lid to reuse again later.

Extensions:

- Add some soft and slow music and this becomes a soothing activity that calms the child.
- Create a pretend city together using rocks for cars and other small objects for trees and houses.
- Add a funnel to encourage controlled pouring.
- Add small cars, trucks, and plastic animals.

Jump Over

Time: 10 to 20 minutes

Materials: Pillows

Preschoolers love to jump, and this activity provides a good workout for a variety of muscles and motor skills, using nothing but pillows. This game encourages your child to do controlled jumps under your watchful eyes. Place the pillows on the grass or indoors on a soft rug. Jump over them from a run of 5 to 6 feet.

Extensions:

- Experiment with different starting distances and talk about how to gain momentum.
- Use a measuring tape to compare jumps.
- Measure your leg lengths and discuss the effect of that number with jumping lengths.

Life-Sized Foil Figures

Time: 20 to 30 minutes

Materials: Scissors, masking tape, heavy-duty aluminum foil

This activity can give your child a whole new perspective on body size. Measure your child's height and cut 2 sheets of foil a bit longer than that length. Tape them together down the center seam. Have your child lie on the floor and place the sheet of foil over them, molding the foil around the arms, legs, torso, and head. Be gentle around the face area. Lift the foil very carefully and trim away the excess. Tack to the wall.

Extensions:

- Let your child help to mold one of you.
- Hang the forms from the ceiling or wall with string.
- Make a mold of a doll or stuffed animal.
- Make molds of other household objects.

Log Roll

Time: 5 to 10 minutes

Materials: Open, grassy area

Your child will love the dizzying effect of this game but will also be challenged to control the body. Have your child lie on her back with her arms extended overhead. In that position, have her roll her body forward in a straight line. Children tend to curl up, so tell her to try to keep her arms above her head and her legs straight. Be sure to take turns and receive feedback on your performance.

Extensions:

- You can add to the challenge substantially if you have a hillside to roll down.
- Try this from the top to the bottom of her bed before a bedtime story.
- On a rainy day, spread out a blanket, and your rolling area will be defined.

Making Flapjacks

Time: 10 to 15 minutes

Materials: Pancake batter, squeeze bottle

Challenge motor control by filling a squeeze bottle with pancake batter and letting your child squirt batter onto the griddle under your careful supervision.

Extensions:

- Drop on raisins, banana circles, carob chips, or minced fruit to create faces or designs.
- Make pancakes shaped like the first letters of your names.
- Pick a number under 10 and make that many small pancakes.
- Make a pancake that is big enough to fill a plate.
- Share the big pancake.

Mirror of Me

Time: 30 minutes to 1 hour

Materials: Shoe-box lid, white glue, small objects (shells, pebbles, miniature toys), small mirror ($), felt pens ($)

Glue a small mirror to the inside lid of a shoe box. Let your child collect small objects from around the house to decorate the mirror and its frame, using glue that is strong enough to hold them in place. Allow to dry thoroughly and finish by decorating with colored felt pens.

Extension:

- Make small mirrors for gifts and customize them by adding names or titles like, "For the Best Dad," "For the Nicest Mom," etc.
- Make several decorated mirrors to hang together for a special "me space."

A Book about Me

Time: 20 to 30 minutes

Materials: White paper, stapler, felt pens ($)

Staple the paper together into a book and talk about what should be included in your child's life story. Include a discussion of the physical similarities to family members to help your child understand his physical inheritance. Review family photos to help generate ideas. Create drawings or staple photos to the paper and write underneath about each one.

Extensions:

- Make this a long-term project and save the pages until the book is ready to be compiled and fastened together with cardboard or a stapled cover.
- Help the child make a book for a grandparent or special family member for a birthday or holiday.

Obstacle Ride

Time: 20 to 30 minutes

Materials: 8 or 9 empty milk cartons or tin cans, chalk ($), bikes or other riding toys ($)

Draw a line about 50 feet long in a clear, paved area. Fill the cans or cartons with sand or rocks and place them alternately about a foot on either side of the line and about 6 feet from each other. Challenge your child to ride on the line without knocking over any of the containers.

Extensions:

- Change the configuration by adding twists and turns and talk about what works and what doesn't.
- Invite friends over and put your child in charge of directing the action.

Shadow Shapes

Time: 15 to 20 minutes

Materials: Bright lamp or floodlight, large pieces of white paper, tape, felt pens ($)

Secure the paper to a wall in layers so that it covers a space from the floor to at least the child's height, with a width of 6 to 8 feet. Darken the room as much as possible by pulling down shades and closing blinds. Plug in the spotlight and direct its beam onto the paper. Have your child stand in front of the light and against the paper, striking a pose. Trace the resulting shadow quickly with a felt pen.

Extensions:

- Continue to copy different poses until the whole paper is filled up with active shapes.
- Color and fill in the shapes with patterns or features.
- Try crouching, stretching, or moving the light closer and farther away.
- Do just a facial profile.

Sock the Ball

Time: 20 to 30 minutes

Materials: String or yarn ($), plastic ball with air holes ($), batting tools like bats or rackets ($)

Suspend the ball at your child's stomach level and take turns hitting it with different tools. Decide which tools work better and see if you can figure out why.

Extensions:

- To make this more challenging, move the ball gently before you swing at it.
- Chart the results.
- Try batting blindfolded, piñata style.

Sticks and Stones

Time: 20 to 30 minutes

Materials: Plastic sandwich bags ($), large mixing bowl, 4 cups of unsweetened cereal ($), 2 cups of pretzel sticks ($), 2 cups of raisins ($)

Good nutrition fuels physical activity, an important concept to reinforce with young children. Measure and pour the ingredients together in a bowl and mix it with clean hands. Pack individual servings into baggies for about 8 cups of a healthy between-meal snack.

Extensions:

- Work together to deliver this snack as gifts to other family members and friends.
- Store a bag of the snack in the car for traveling.

Tip-Toes

Time: 5 to 10 minutes

Materials: None

This simple activity can help to develop good balance and spatial awareness. Take off your shoes and stand together on the tip of your toes for as long as possible.

Extensions:

- Repeat, wearing shoes and talk about the difference.
- Experiment by holding arms out at the sides and discuss if it helps or not.
- Bend forward while on tiptoes.
- Time your efforts and chart them, seeing if you can improve your records.
- Try standing on one foot and then the other.

Toss It

Time: 15 to 20 minutes

Materials: 4 or 5 empty boxes, bikes or other riding toys ($), 4 to 5 sealable plastic baggies ($), dried beans ($)

Beanbags can be made by putting dry beans into doubled up ziplock baggies. Arrange the empty boxes in a zigzag pattern about 8 feet apart. Challenge the bike riders to travel through the course, dropping a beanbag into each box while riding past.

Extensions:

- Run or skip past the boxes and drop a beanbag into each box without stopping.
- Put the boxes further apart and then closer together.
- Marbles ($) or small balls ($) can be substituted for the beanbags.

Tracing

Time: 10 to 20 minutes

Materials: Paper, pencil

To help prepare for writing, you can strengthen motor skills by tracing over simple lines and designs. Draw simple shapes on plain paper and cover with a second sheet so your child can practice following the lines.

Extensions:

- Trace simple pictures from a coloring book.
- Trace around the hand or foot.
- Trace something very big (as big as you can find paper for) and something very small.

Walk My Walk

Time: 15 to 20 minutes

Materials: None

Take turns challenging each other to walk like a particular person might, such as a tightrope walker, astronaut on the moon, window washer on a high ledge, old person, baby learning to walk, circus clown, marching soldier, etc. In addition to sparking the imagination, this activity involves a great deal of controlled movement.

Extensions:

- Do the same game but move backwards.
- Repeat, using animal movements.
- Take your child to see a real mime performance ($).

Zigzag Run

Time: 10 to 20 minutes

Materials: Items for an obstacle course, such as cones, boxes, chairs, or masking tape

Set up a running obstacle course that will require rapid shifts of the body so you get a sense of quick movements and precision.

Extensions:

- After running the course a few times, make up new directions like walk around the chair, jump to the chalk line, run back to the blocks, etc.
- For indoors, mark the floor path with masking tape on the floor and run without touching each other.
- Use fast and then slow music to guide your movements.

Aimed Long Shots

Time: 20 minutes

Materials: 2 cones or other markers, playground ball ($)

Precision is the task you will work on with this activity. Mark a goal 6 to 8 feet wide to use for a target, and take turns aiming and kicking a ball that is laid on the ground so it lands between them. To assure success, the goal can be widened and the kicking distance shortened.

Extensions:

- Roll the ball slowly toward the kicker.
- Try distance kicking by aiming in the general area of a target.
- Use balls of various sizes.

Blowing in the Wind

Time: 15 to 20 minutes

Materials: Several strips of lightweight fabric cut 3 to 4 feet long

This is another simple tool to encourage running. Cut a slit in the end of the strips of fabric and slide them onto your child's upper or lower arm. Attach 2 to 4 to each arm and head outside on a breezy day to move and run.

Extensions:

- Head down a hill for a flying effect.
- Make headbands by tying behind the head with ends trailing.
- Add to the knees or waist, which will require more vigorous running to get them flapping.

Body Sounds

Time: 10 minutes

Materials: None

This activity encourages your child to see bodies from a different point of view. Work together to come up with a list of all the sounds you can think of that you can make with your bodies. Your list could include things like clicking, finger snapping, clapping, toe tapping, whistling, etc.

Extensions:

- Write the sounds down and take turns picking one and doing it.
- Talk about the sounds we make that are not polite in public. Discuss why they are necessary to the body even though they are not polite in public.
- Practice learning to whistle.

Bouncing

Time: 20 to 30 minutes

Materials: Rubber playground ball ($)

Bouncing and catching a ball is a good way to start your child off in ball skills. Hold the ball with both hands and drop it to the ground. When it bounces up, push it down again with a quick push. Discourage bending to meet the ball.

Extensions:

- After some practice, challenge your child to do this with one hand.
- Try passing the ball to each other, allowing it to bounce only once.
- Practice passing the ball back and forth from the left hand to the right.

Designer Helmets

Time: 10 to 15 minutes

Materials: Brightly colored plastic tape ($), bicycle helmet ($)

Wearing a helmet is essential for protecting your child from head trauma, but you can help to make it more fun by making the helmet fancy. Offer strips of colored plastic tape to create stick-on lightning bolts, personal initials, or racing stripes.

Extension:

- If your child has neighborhood friends, they can make matching team helmets.

Festive Bike Frames

Time: 15 to 20 minutes

Materials: Empty paper-towel tubes, brightly colored plastic tape ($)

You can assure lots of bike riding by helping your child to jazz up bikes with a row of slip-on fringe. Wrap colored plastic tape around a cardboard paper towel tube. Add individual streamers by sticking one end of a 10-inch piece of tape to the tube. Fold the hanging portion of the tape in half, pressing the sticky sides together. Use scissors to cut the length of the tube so that the cylinder can be slipped onto the frame.

Healthy Nachos

Time: 10 minutes

Materials: Corn tortillas ($), grated low-fat cheese ($)

With this activity it's fun to cook a simple, healthy food to fuel active play and to help your child learn grown up tasks. Cut corn tortillas into 6 triangles and sprinkle with grated low-fat cheese. Bake at 350 degrees until the tortillas are crisp and the cheese is melted.

Extensions:

- Add other healthy ingredients like nonfat refried beans, olive slices, or chopped tomatoes.
- Leave the tortilla whole and top with the ingredients before baking. Remove from the oven and add chopped lettuce and tomato for a taco salad.

Hip Hubcaps

Time: 20 to 30 minutes

Materials: Colorful drinking straws ($), craft knife ($)

Give bikes a new look that encourages use by decorating the spokes. Use the craft knife (adults only) to make a cut down the length of each straw and slip them over a bike-wheel spoke. Repeat for each spoke.

I Can Do It Myself

Time: 15 to 20 minutes

Materials: Large piece of cardboard, magazine pictures, felt pens ($)

We are each responsible for our own health—an important lesson to learn at an early age. Make up a list of healthy responsibilities on a piece of cardboard, using pictures cut or drawn from magazines. Include such things as, "I take a bath," "I wear clean clothes," "I brush my teeth," "I wash my hands before eating," "I brush my hair," and "I eat fruits and vegetables." Make check-off boxes next to each item and review together at the end of the day.

Extensions:

- Add a reward for special achievements, like completing a difficult or disliked task.
- Add a bonus task that is mutually agreed upon, along with a reasonable reward.
- Work together to make a list for you to stick to.
- Put a sticker ($) by each task that is completed.

Juiced Up

Time: 15 to 20 minutes

Materials: Fruit like oranges, grapefruit, or lemons; sugar; water; drinking glasses; juicer and strainer (optional)

Healthy bodies don't run well on soda. Let your child enjoy the fruits of their labors by experience. Extract juice from the fruits by squeezing pieces of fruit that have been cut in half. Strain, if desired, although the pulp is full of nutritious vitamins. Add enough sugar and water to match your preferred taste.

Extensions:

- If you can have some purchased juice available, do a taste test of fresh versus prepared.
- Use a blindfold and run a taste test on family or friends.
- Read the vitamin content on the purchased container and talk about what it means.

Letters for Lunch

Time: 10 to 15 minutes

Materials: Lunch food items

This activity gives you an opening to talk about good nutrition and put it into practice in a playful way. Pick a letter of the alphabet and plan a lunch that contains only food items that begin with that letter. For example, a "B" lunch could have a bologna sandwich, banana, and box of gingersnaps.

Extensions:

- Plan a meal that has foods that begin with the initials from your names.
- Plan a meal with 3 letters that spell something, such as *yum*.

Lunch Menus

Time: 10 to 15 minutes

Materials: Sandwich fillings, fruits, vegetables, drinks, snacks

Reinforce good nutrition and eliminate mealtime battles by writing down a menu full of choices that can be used to prepare for lunch. Include category headings like "Select a Sandwich," "Pick a Fruit," "Choose a Vegetable," "Pick a Drink," and "Vote for a Treat." List healthy choices under each category so your child can circle them as the lunch is designed.

Extensions:

- Create a similar menu for breakfast or snacks.
- Plan lunch for the family by using this list to poll them on their choices.

Mirror Partner

Time: 10 to 15 minutes

Materials: None

This activity involves recognizing how the body moves. Face each other. One of you is the leader and moves a part of the body slowly. The other copies the action as closely as possible before exchanging roles.

Extensions:

- Speed up or slow down your actions by adding music.
- Try doing this activity outdoors, where it will seem more natural to make large body movements.
- Wear props like hats and coats that can be tipped, put on, and removed.

Precise Jumping and Landing

Time: 15 to 20 minutes

Materials: Old tires

Use the arms for balance as you jump on and off the tire surfaces until you get comfortable with the motion. Encourage landing on both feet.

Extensions:

- Once confidence is achieved, try jumping from one tire to another.
- Reverse directions or go backward.
- Make up a routine and take turns doing it properly.
- Use a timer.
- A small exercise trampoline ($) can be substituted for the tires.

Ready to Play

Time: 20 to 30 minutes

Materials: Basic sports equipment of any kind ($)

Confidence grows when your grade-school child feels skilled at basic sports. You can help to build those skills even if you can only work out once a week. Focus on learning to throw, catch, and kick balls properly. Help with the concept of following through with the arms and body weight when swinging or batting. Teach your child to step forward when throwing at a target and to build endurance by slowly jogging a regular, reasonable distance that builds over time.

Extensions:

- Attend a high school or little league game to stimulate interest with live action.
- Mark regular practice sessions on a calendar so your child can anticipate them as special times.
- Go out together to watch a sport that your child is not familiar with, like golf, tennis, or archery.

Run for It

Time: 15 to 30 minutes

Materials: None

After a few stretches to get warmed up, head out together for a healthy run. Beginners should alternate a 2-minute jog with a 1-minute walk for a total of 15 minutes. Intermediate runners can alternate a 4-minute jog with a 1-minute walk for a total of 15 to 20 minutes. When you are advanced, you can jog for 10 to 15 minutes straight.

Extension:

- Go to a high school track on the weekend or evening and do a lap there.
- Use a pedometer ($) to measure steps. Compare the numbers for each of your strides.

Spinners

Time: 20 to 30 minutes

Materials: Yard of string or yarn ($), wooden rectangle approximately 2 inches by 1 inch by ½ inch ($), drill with a ⅛-inch bit ($), staple gun ($), strips of colored crepe paper ($)

Simple tools can be made to encourage running and active play. For this tool, drill a ⅛-inch hole at one end of the wood. Slip the string through the hole and tie tightly. Staple several strips of crepe paper at the other end. Have your child hold the string in his hand and run.

Extensions:

- Use one in each hand and run to a designated spot and back.
- Use music to jazz things up.
- Spin it around in a circle for a flash of moving color.

Tube Trials

Time: 20 to 30 minutes

Materials: 6 carpet tubes (carpet stores are usually happy to save them for you), hand saw (adults only)

If you can get some of the recycled tubes from a store nearby, they make a terrific obstacle course for running. Cut each tube in half so that you have a dozen pieces, each about 2 to 3 feet long. Arrange them in a row outside, about a foot apart, where there is lots of room to run. Take turns running through the tubes without touching them.

Extensions:

- For variety, spread the tubes further apart or put them closer together.
- Paint the tubes in bright colors ($) and take turns yelling out directions according to colors. For example, "Jump over blue backwards and go around orange."

Walk the Wire

Time: 20 to 30 minutes

Materials: Piece of rope at least 12 feet long ($)

With a little imagination, this balancing act can take on its own drama. Stretch a rope piece across an outdoor surface (asphalt or grass) and tie the ends to fences or trees so it is taut across the ground. To walk the "high wire," place the heel of one foot over the starting line and begin to walk, placing the heel of one foot directly in front of the toe of the other foot. Continue all the way across the rope, keeping the arms out for balance.

Extensions:

- Give this a try in stocking-feet or bare feet.
- Go backward when forward movement is mastered.
- See how slow and how fast you can go.
- Count the maximum number of steps that can be taken before falling off.

It is tempting to think of playfulness as icing on the cake, particularly if you compare it to the other six skills listed in this book. But picture adults who work long hours, complain of stress, and have high blood pressure, and its value is more obvious. Playfulness is an antidote to life's ills and a key to enjoying life's rewards. Although play is natural for children, the attitude and habit of playfulness must be continually observed and experienced to keep it as a lifelong habit.

When you model playfulness in times of turmoil, boredom, or distress, you teach useful coping mechanisms and healthy options for turning difficult situations into positive outcomes. Seeing that joking and laughter are acceptable remedies for dealing with stress is a valuable lesson, and, best of all, you get to share the fun of working through difficulties together with a minimum of disruption.

Life today is fast-lane and stressful, even for children. The playful child has the advantage of being able to switch gears and find alternatives when life is too full or things don't go as planned. The playful child is creative and fun to be with, which enhances popularity. They know how to use humor as a play tool and to forgive and forget as a matter of course.

In the activities in this chapter, you can teach your child playfulness through bouts of silliness, shared good times, laughter, joking, and a tickle here and there. You can surprise your child with unexpected ways of doing things together as you encourage keeping difficulties in perspective and maintaining control so that life remains enjoyable.

Back and Forth

Time: 5 to 10 minutes

Materials: Hand-sized objects

This game helps your baby to understand your separateness. Hand the objects back and forth, talking about what you are doing.

Extensions:

- Take all of the objects, then give them all back in a big flurry.
- Hand them out, saying, "One for me and one for you."

Chase Me

Time: 5 to 10 minutes

Materials: None

Once your baby can crawl, chasing is great fun that brings reams of laughter. Get down on your hands and knees and move toward your baby, exclaiming, "I'm going to catch you."

Extensions:

- Challenge your baby to chase you.
- Use a doll or stuffed animal to do the chasing.
- Give a doll to your baby and keep one for yourself, taking turns to let the dolls chase each other until you both collapse into a pile of laughs and giggles.

More and More Hats

Time: 5 to 10 minutes

Materials: Half a dozen or more hats

Sit on the floor with a basketful of hats and put them on your head, one at a time. Pass one to your baby to put on and keep taking turns with the different hats.

Extensions:

- Play this in front of a mirror.
- Change your voice each time you change a hat.
- Wear 2 hats at a time.
- Put some hats on bears, dolls, and stuffed animals.

Pillow Fun

Time: 5 to 10 minutes

Materials: Small pile of pillows

This activity needs little more than your encouragement to provide giggles and smiles. Pile the pillows in the middle of the floor and put your baby on top of them. Fluff the pillows around her body so it feels soft and talk about what you are doing as you play.

Extensions:

- Cover your baby (except for her face) with pillows so the soft weight is felt.
- Fluff a small pillow on your tummy and then on your baby's. Repeat gently with other body parts as you talk about what you are doing.
- Gently roll your baby across the pillows.

Silly Stuff

Time: 5 minutes

Materials: Common household items

To encourage the development of humor, notice what your baby finds funny and repeat it. Try shaking your head and talking in a funny voice. Generally, anything out of the ordinary will make babies laugh as long as it is not startling or loud.

Extensions:

- Add props like hats, glasses, and other things that change your appearance.
- Try the props on your baby in front of a mirror and laugh together.
- Pretend to drink out of a baby bottle.
- Creep your fingers up his arm and around his other body parts.

Water Play

Time: 30 minutes

Materials: Wading or plastic tub with a few inches of water, waterplay equipment such as empty squeeze bottles, plastic cups, boats, funnels, balls, floating objects, plant sprayer, sponge or dish rag, etc.

Babies love water, and you won't need to give them directions except to set out the water and get playful. Add anything that seems interesting. Remember to *never* leave your baby unattended, even for a few moments.

Extensions:

- Add a few drops of scented extract, such as lemon or peppermint.
- Add a few drops of food coloring.
- Add a small amount of baby shampoo and work up some bubbles with your hands.
- Pat the water with your hands so it splashes.

Baby Boogie

Time: 5 to 10 minutes

Materials: None

Toddlers can try your patience, and using playful fun can often turn the tide. An unhappy toddler can often be distracted by something as simple as your singing as you pick them up and dance around to some lively music.

Extensions:

- Hold hands and dance together across the floor.
- Add some rhythmic clapping to the dance.
- Dance together in front of a mirror.

Belly Buttons

Time: 5 minutes

Materials: None

Tummies are always playful areas for tickling and nuzzling. With this game, you use bath time to point out your toddler's belly button and push it gently with a little "honk."

Extensions:

- Show that you have a belly button and "honk" it.
- Cover her belly button with a washcloth and let her take it on and off so you can "honk" her belly button when it is exposed.

DIRT AND MUD PLAY

Time: 15 to 30 minutes

Materials: Patch of dirt, spoon or small trowel, water, small stick

Strip your toddler down to a diaper or put on a swimsuit, and work together in the shade by playing with mud. Once you locate a small patch of bare dirt, begin digging, using the trowel, spoon, or stick. Add a small amount of water and model mixing it together with the hands. This activity is a guaranteed winner.

Extensions:

- Add a plastic cup or carton to spoon dirt and mud into.
- Add plastic little people or animals.
- Add a little coarse sand so the texture changes.
- Add small broken twigs and hand-sized rocks.

FACE PAINTING

Time: 5 to 20 minutes

Materials: 1 teaspoon cornstarch, food coloring ($), ½ teaspoon water, 1½ teaspoons cold cream ($), small paper cups ($), small paintbrush ($)

Face painting is play at its best, and this simple recipe also cleans up easily due to the cold cream. Mix together the cornstarch, water, and cold cream in a small paper cup. Add a few drops of food coloring and apply to the face in designs or small pictures (flowers, butterflies, hearts...) using a toothpick or small brush.

Extensions:

- Take your traveling make-up kit on the road and offer your services to other family and friends.
- Make a list of simple things to paint on faces, or make samples that your toddler can choose from.

Funny Biscuits

Time: 10 to 15 minutes

Materials: Tube of refrigerated roll dough ($)

Eating these whimsical biscuits when they are done adds to the fun. Using the hands, flatten, roll, and shape the dough into new shapes before baking.

Extensions:

- Shape into simple animals and add raisins for eyes.
- Flatten into circles and paint on faces using egg yolk mixed with food coloring.
- Sprinkle with powdered sugar or coconut for snowballs.

Megaphone

Time: 10 to 15 minutes

Materials: Empty paper-towel tube

Voices can be funny and your toddler will enjoy experimenting with voice modulation. Use the tube to experiment with your voices, changing the pitch and loudness to demonstrate the possibilities.

Extensions:

- Use 2 megaphones so you can take turns talking with your toddler.
- Vary the tone of your voice and encourage your toddler to do the same.
- Use your toddler's name as you talk.
- Encourage your toddler to say his name, sing a song, or make animal noises with the tube.
- Tap your 2 megaphones together to make a totally new sound.

Monkey Business

Time: 10 to 15 minutes

Materials: Large piece of foam or old mattress

Toddlers love to jump, an activity that helps them learn a great deal about what their bodies can and cannot do. A jumping pad or mattress provides a safe place to jump, fall, roll, tumble, and practice emerging moving skills while having a playful time burning off energy.

Extensions:

- Have your toddler jump into your arms as you stand close to the side.
- Have your toddler jump while holding a favorite doll or stuffed animal.
- Add some pillows on the center of the mattress.

Puddle Jumping

Time: 5 to 10 minutes

Materials: Puddles after a rainy day or a lawn watering

Being told that it is OK to jump in puddles will bring squeals of delight. Go out together dressed in rain gear and stomp in the puddles.

Extensions:

- Model dragging your feet gently through the water.
- Play "follow the leader" as you play in the water.
- Hold hands and jump with both feet into shallow puddles.

Smashing Towers

Time: 5 to 10 minutes

Materials: Set of small table blocks ($)

Toddlers enjoy knocking things down as much as building them. Make a tower of blocks and tip it over together with a gentle and slow movement.

Extensions:

- Make several towers next to each other.
- Stack canned goods, shoes, and anything else that can be safely piled up.

Taxi

Time: 5 to 10 minutes

Materials: Two chairs

Pretend play can begin during the toddler stage if you lead the way. Place the chairs side by side and pretend you are the taxi driver. Ask your toddler where to go, giving suggestions, if needed. Talk about all the things you pretend to see along the way and talk about what you will do when you get there.

Extensions:

- Let your toddler drive and pick where you will go.
- Use a plate (preferably plastic or paper for lightness) for a steering wheel.
- Add a chair behind and throw toys and other belongings in the back seat.
- Put chairs in a line so you can drive a train.

Teddy Bear Tickle

Time: 5 to 10 minutes

Materials: Favorite teddy bear or other stuffed animal

Tickling is fun and this activity prepares the child for a few mutual tickles between you afterward. Using a favorite teddy bear or stuffed animal, point to, name, and tickle the different body parts of the stuffed animal as you call them out.

Extensions:

- A simpler version would be for you to name the parts and have your toddler tickle that part; then you tickle that part on your toddler.
- Tickle a bear part and the same part on your toddler.

Tissue Fun

Time: 5 to 10 minutes

Materials: Box of nose tissues

It is always fun to be able to do the unexpected. Give the half-empty box to your toddler to pull out the tissues while you need a few minutes to finish something of your own.

Extensions:

- Roll the tissues into balls and play silly games with them, such as bouncing them off the head or batting them in the air.
- Get on the floor and blow the tissues about.
- Throw tissues at each other, saying, "It doesn't hurt!"
- Pretend to sneeze and blow your nose.

What's in a Name

Time: 5 to 10 minutes

Materials: None

Set the stage for fun by inserting your toddler's name as the main character of a familiar song. For example, "Happy Lucy had a farm, ee-i-ee-i-oh...," or "Bobby goes 'round the mulberry bush..."

Extensions:

- Make up a song based on something your toddler is doing at the moment and incorporate her name into it.
- Do the same thing with your own name.
- Ask your toddler who else she would like to sing about and work that name into a song.
- Have a pretend birthday party and sing the birthday song to the birthday guest.

Wallow in Paper

Time: 5 to 10 minutes

Materials: Newspaper

This silly game is perfect for prebath time, particularly if your toddler is tired and not cooperating. Get a stack of newspapers and pull out sheets to crumple and throw into a pile together. When you are done, move on to the bathtub to clean up.

Extensions:

- Throw wads of crumpled paper at each other.
- Put the crumpled paper into paper grocery bags, squishing them down as you go.
- Let your toddler roll around in the wadded pile of paper and tickle her as she does so.

Belt It Out

Time: 15 to 30 minutes

Materials: None

Singing is a tremendous self-esteem booster and it's fun to do together. Begin with songs that have a chorus, like "Old Macdonald," and belt it out to model how fun this can be. Try it in the car, while washing dishes, or while cooking together.

Extensions:

- Make up a silly song about something your child is wearing or doing.
- Encourage your child make up a song about you or what you are doing.

Colored Glue Art

Time: 5 minutes

Materials: Glue, food coloring ($), empty detergent squeeze bottles

Colored glue makes craft projects more fun, and this recipe can save you from purchasing the expensive commercial brands. If you buy the white glue in bulk, you will save even more. Add a few drops of food coloring, stir, and place in recycled squeeze bottles for squirting onto art projects.

Extensions:

- Add some scented extract that goes with the color, like strawberry for red.
- Use the colored glue to create designs by dripping it onto dark paper.

Corny Pictures

Time: 10 to 15 minutes

Materials: Paper, several pieces of cooked and cooled corn on the cob ($), paint ($)

It may strike your child as very silly to use food to paint. Dip the cooled corn in the paint and roll it around on the paper for a new kind of painting experience.

Extensions:

- Try the same thing with uncooked corn and compare the results.
- Make prints by stamping with the end.
- Drop some of the corn silk on the wet paint and let it dry in place.
- Wash your hands and butter up a fresh piece for a snack.

Easy Water Balloons

Time: 15 to 20 minutes

Materials: Bucket of water, plastic sandwich bags

This activity provides a fun way for cooling off on a hot day. Fill the bucket with water. Dip the bags in and fill and seal them shut before tossing them back and forth like water balloons.

Extensions:

- Toss the bags hard onto the ground for a quick splash.
- Pick a target and do target practice.
- See how high each of you can throw.
- See how far each of you can throw.

Eat Your Vegetables

Time: 10 to 15 minutes

Materials: Crackers or a slice of bread, peanut butter, grated carrots or zucchini, small plastic picnic knife ($)

If you have a child who doesn't like vegetables, get playful and spread peanut butter on a cracker or slice of bread and then let the child top it with grated carrot or zucchini. This makes eating vegetables fun.

Extensions:

- Add a few nuts or raisins.
- Top with cucumber or celery slices.
- Search the kitchen together to find things to put on top, being inventive and open-minded.

Jump Over the River

Time: 20 to 30 minutes

Materials: Area outside with sand or dirt, water

This activity calls for a bit of daring and a few splashes. Dig a pit a few inches deep and a few feet across. Fill with water and take turns jumping barefooted across it.

Extensions:

- Use a smooth board for a plank to walk across with the arms out for balance.
- Walk directly through the water, enjoying the coolness.

Magic Sandwiches

Time: 15 to 30 minutes

Materials: Wide-rimmed glass, bread, sandwich fillings, food coloring ($), milk, small paintbrush ($)

Why eat ordinary sandwiches when you can have magically colored ones? Begin by cutting the bread into a circle, using the glass. Mix a small amount of milk with food coloring and paint designs lightly onto the bread, making sure that is does not become soaked. Toast the bread before making sandwiches.

Extensions:

- Sprinkle the colors with cinnamon before toasting and use it for a tea party.
- Let your child make a sandwich for you after asking you questions to guide choices.
- Use a color theme, like all red or red and yellow, for creating a sandwich.
- Use cookie cutters ($) to make fanciful sandwich shapes.

Mirror Play

Time: 15 to 30 minutes

Materials: Mirror, dry-erase pen ($)

You can make yourself look silly with new features without any mess if you try this activity. Stand very still in front of a mirror and use the dry-erase pen to add features on your reflections by drawing on it. You may want to add freckles, red hair, a clown hat, or a big nose.

Extensions:

- Make your child's reflection into an animal face.
- Squeeze close together and do features on both of your faces at the same time.

Mud Pies for Sale

Time: 20 to 30 minutes

Materials: Dirt or sand, water

Find a comfortable place to sit by some dirt or sand and mix up a batch with the hands. Scoop and mold into smooth pies and set out to dry in the sun. The next step is to open your pretend bakery.

Extensions:

- Add twigs for birthday candles and celebrate a pretend birthday.
- Sprinkle with dry sand or dirt for sugar cookies.
- Decorate with pebbles and leaves.
- Take turns buying and selling the treats to each other.

My Own Jewelry

Time: 10 to 20 minutes

Materials: String, tape, plastic straws ($)

This personal jewelry is fun to make. Wrap the end of a string with a piece of tape so it is slightly smaller than the hole in the straw. Cut the straws into pieces from ½ to 1 inch in length. Tie the string around the first piece and string on the remainder, leaving enough string to tie the ends together.

Extensions:

- Use thick elastic string for stretchable necklaces, bracelets, and anklets.
- Hang lengths of string as decoration.
- Make matching jewelry for a stuffed animal or doll.

Shadow Tag

Time: 5 to 10 minutes

Materials: None

This is an old game of tag, but always one that brings laughter. Go out into the sun and take turns jumping on each other's shadows. Run and hide your own shadow in other shadows. Make pretend "Ouch!" cries when you are caught.

Extensions:

- Reverse rolls.
- Play on a grassy area where you can run hard.
- Make your shadows hug and make up when you are finished stomping.

Splatters Everywhere

Time: 10 to 20 minutes

Materials: Paper, 4 small blocks of wood or 4 bricks, piece of screen (with taped edges to prevent cutting) ($), paint ($), paintbrush ($)

Spread plenty of newspaper on the surrounding area and wear old shirts or aprons, as this activity is fun but messy. Suspend the screen over the paper by setting it on the four blocks or bricks. Paint across the screen so that the paint splatters down onto the paper.

Extensions:

- Substitute a toothbrush for the paintbrush.
- Place an object, such as a leaf, on the paper and the splattering will leave its outline when it is removed.
- Use several colors and allow it to dry so it can be used for wrapping paper.

Sugared Chalk

Time: 15 to 20 minutes

Materials: ⅓ cup sugar, 1 cup water, colored chalk ($), black paper ($)

This activity is irresistibly fun because the colors become more brilliant and smudge less due to the added sugar crystals. Mix the sugar and water until dissolved and place the chalk sticks into the solution for 5 to 10 minutes. It is not necessary to let them dry before using them to draw on the paper.

Extensions:

- Use other kinds of paper like brown grocery bags or white paper.
- Try it out on pieces of fabric.
- Try it outside on the sidewalk.

Water Squeeze

Time: 15 to 20 minutes

Materials: An empty detergent squeeze bottle, water

It is the novelty in this activity that makes it appealing. Remove unnecessary clothing and take a squeeze bottle full of water outside to shoot and squirt in any way and at anything.

Extensions:

- Provide squeeze bottles with different colors of water in them, made by adding a drop of food coloring.
- Add some baby shampoo for bubbles.
- Make chalk pictures ($) on the pavement to erase using the squeeze bottle.

Whale in the Bath

Time: 15 to 20 minutes

Materials: Empty plastic milk-gallon carton or juice jug, scissors, permanent marker

This creature of the deep can make bath time more appealing and fun. Turn the jug on its side so that the handle is on top and draw a mouth shape on the base of the jug, extending partway up the sides. Cut along the line. Using the marker, outline the edge of the mouth and add eyes and a blowhole. The whale scoop is ready for swimming, scooping and sinking into the deepest parts of the bathtub.

Extensions:

- Add some small plastic fish for the whale to gobble up.
- Let the whale clean up the bath toys when it is time to get out.

Apple Candlesticks

Time: 20 to 30 minutes

Materials: Paring knife, plastic wrap, potato peeler, lemon juice, 2 Rome Beauty apples ($), 2 candles ($)

You will probably want an extra apple to cut up and eat as you make these attractive table decorations. Core the apple halfway into the center to make room for the candles. Use plastic wrap around the base if the hole is too large. Carve designs into the apple skin, using the potato peeler. Rub the exposed apple with lemon juice to keep it from discoloring.

Extensions:

- Carve designs for specific holidays or parties.
- Use candles that match the apples.

Bug Prints

Time: 30 minutes

Materials: White paper, pencil, inkpad ($)

Your child has probably never taken a close look at fingerprints, let alone used them for play. Set out the paper and make fingerprints using an inkpad. Use a pencil to add legs and antennae to the prints so they look like bugs.

Extensions:

- Use larger sheets of white shelf paper and you have unique and artsy wrapping paper.
- Draw in rocks and branches for the bugs to sit on.
- Fold paper in half and decorate the front with bugs for note cards.
- Cut long pieces of cardboard or construction paper to make buggy bookmarks.

Bugs on a Log

Time: 10 to 15 minutes

Materials: Stalks of celery, peanut butter or cheese spread ($), raisins ($), small plastic picnic knife ($)

Wash the celery and cut it into logs about 5 to 8 inches long. Use the plastic knife to spread the peanut butter or cheese in the cavity. Add bugs by placing the raisins onto the peanut butter. Eat and enjoy together, or share your silly snack with other family members.

Extensions:

- For a special treat, use carob chips for bugs.
- Grate on some carrot or sprinkle with coconut for worms on a log.

Crazy Furniture

Time: 20 to 30 minutes

Materials: A few pieces of lightweight outdoor furniture

Redefine the ordinary world into something more playful by moving the regular furniture to the sides of a room and bringing in some outdoor furniture for a movie or to read books.

Extensions:

- Turn a piece of furniture on its side and have your child suggest new ways to use it.
- Add pillows, towels, and blankets.
- Drape the new additions with sheets.

Cup of Worms

Time: 5 to 10 minutes

Materials: Clear glasses or cups, chocolate pudding ($), candied jelly worms ($), cocoa powder ($)

Here is a playful party treat perfectly suited to preschool humor. Make the pudding together and spoon it into clear cups before cooling it in the refrigerator. Top it with a few candy worms and sprinkle with a little cocoa powder (dirt) on the top for a very playful snack of dirt dessert.

Extensions:

- Add worms to the sides of the clear plastic cups before adding the pudding so you can see the worms underground.
- Add some grated coconut for baby worms.

Eggbeater

Time: 5 to 10 minutes

Materials: Plastic tub or bowl, liquid detergent, hand-cranked eggbeater ($)

The eggbeater is a tool that is safe, noisy, and fun to use. Fill the tub with water and add a squirt of liquid detergent. Then step back and let your child experience the fun of a hand-generated motor.

Extensions:

- Add a drop of yellow food coloring to one side of the tub and a drop of red to the other.
- Use real eggs to beat, and cook them after they are beaten to a frothy stage

Got Monsters?

Time: 15 to 30 minutes

Materials: Storybooks about monsters, such as *Where the Wild Things Are* by Maurice Sendak, *There's a Nightmare in My Closet* by Mercer Mayer, *Dorrie the Witch* by Patricia Coombs, or *Georgie* by Robert Bright ($)

Bedtime monsters and other scary things can be all too real for preschoolers with active imaginations. Try reading one of these classic monster books to help your child laugh and work through the issues.

Extensions:

- Draw pictures of monsters together and talk about their features.
- Purchase a monster or dinosaur doll ($) and use it to talk about and act out imaginary situations.

Indoor Hide and Seek

Time: 10 to 20 minutes

Materials: Household objects

If it is too late in the day to play outdoors or the weather is bad, you can pass some time by hiding an object in the house and using simple clues to help find it. For example, use category clues like, "It is not in a room with a sink," or, "It is close to the floor."

Extensions:

- Hide a treat and enjoy it together when it is found.
- Hide coupons to a movie or restaurant.
- Hide coupons good for a kiss and hug.

Loud and Soft Melodies

Time: 10 to 20 minutes

Materials: None

Playing with voice control leaves lots of room for getting silly. Begin by singing a song together, and as you go, alternate between quiet and loud, taking turns calling the directions.

Extensions:

- When you sing softly, squat low, and when you sing loudly, stand up on the tiptoes with the arms wide open.
- Alternate loud and soft singing between the two of you.

Noodle Fun

Time: 15 to 20 minutes

Materials: Paper, glue, dry pasta in as many shapes as possible ($)

Using pasta in this unusual way will make your child more aware of sizes and shapes. Cover a sheet of paper with a thin layer of white glue, spreading it with the fingers. Wash hands and then arrange pieces of dry pasta on top of the glue. Let dry thoroughly before lifting and hanging up for display.

Extensions:

- Make sure the edges of all pieces touch when glued and pry them off the paper in a single sheet when they are dry. You can spray paint the dried creation and hang it from a string.
- Cover a cardboard box or empty food container with pasta package. You can use this as a package for gifts.

Oily Dough

Time: 15 to 20 minutes

Materials: Flour, oil, water

This is an easy dough to make, and it has a nice slippery consistency. Mix 4 cups of flour with a cup each of water and oil. Knead to desired consistency for molding, adding flour until no longer sticky. Experiment with rolling, squishing, and molding this slimy dough.

Extensions:

- Make with pleasantly warm water.
- Add color or scents.
- Coil into ropes to wind into cups or simple dishes.

Paint-a-Thon

Time: 30 to 40 minutes

Materials: Paper; assorted objects to paint with, such as golf balls, bottle caps, cans, toy cars, feathers, forks, leaves, keys, pine needles, poster paint ($)

Painting has never been more playful than in this activity. Set out a few of the items and experiment by dipping them into the paint one at a time and printing the images on the paper. Add and remove items as you go along.

Extensions:

- Walk around the house and find additional items to use, talking about why they might or might not be good choices. Talk about what happens when you try each one.
- Sit down to study the art when it is dry and identify the tool used for each, if possible.
- Discuss which tools were easier, more fun, disappointing, etc.

Painting Rocks

Time: Collecting time plus 15 to 20 minutes

Materials: Medium-sized rocks collected on a walk, tempera paints ($), paintbrushes ($)

Get playful, and when you look at the rock shapes together, you can see familiar shapes that you can use to paint faces, features, or just designs. Sign each one that you create as a custom work of art.

Extensions:

- Arrange the finished rocks into a rock garden for permanent display.
- Add a sprinkle of glitter ($) for a special effect.
- Use glue ($) to bond several rocks together to make more complex creations.

Silly Rhymes

Time: 10 to 20 minutes

Materials: None

Walking together provides the perfect setting for word games. The next time you are out walking, take turns picking out objects to rhyme real words to. For example, *tree: me, flea, bee, three, see*. Move on to the next object when neither of you can think of any more rhyming words.

Extensions:

- Use your names and those of others you know to begin rhymes.
- Take turns thinking of words and songs that use them.

Stomp and Pop

Time: 10 minutes

Materials: String, scissors, balloons ($)

Blow up a balloon and tie a piece of string on it about 18 inches long. Tie the other end around your ankles and hop about as you try to pop each other's balloons.

Extensions:

- Put a balloon behind your back and try to pop it against the wall.
- Use a thumbtack to pop balloons, counting to 3 before popping so you are both ready.
- Take turns calling out a color and popping just balloons of that color.

Storybook Tea Party

Time: 20 to 30 minutes

Materials: Tea, snacks, dishes

On the next rainy day, indulge in some fantasy with a tea party right out of your child's favorite storybook. Pick a favorite book and assign characters. For example, you might want to be the animals in *Charlotte's Web*. Talk about things the characters would know and do before the party begins.

Extension:

- Use costumes or hats to make pretending even easier.

Summertime Magic Ale

Time: 5 to 10 minutes

Materials: Blue food coloring ($), clear glasses or cups, lemonade ($)

Here is a treat that will not only be welcomed on a hot day, but which will spark play and conversation as well. Add blue food coloring to the water before freezing it into ice cubes. Add the blue ice cubes to glasses of lemonade and watch what happens as it melts. As the colors in this summertime drink change, your child will be amazed.

Extensions:

- For even more color, make some bright yellow cubes and add them along with a blue cube.
- Freeze a few blueberries or other small pieces of fruit into the cubes for an extra treat.

Tracing Shadows

Time: 10 to 15 minutes

Materials: Chalk ($)

Stand in the full sun and have your child strike a pose. Quickly trace the shadow with chalk.

Extension:

- Strike different poses.
- Return to the same place several hours later and repeat. Talk about what happened to the shadows.
- Color in features and clothing.
- Throw water on the pictures to erase them and begin again.
- Trace the shadows of other objects.

Upside-Down Picnic

Time: 30 minutes

Materials: Table, sheet, picnic lunch or dinner

Instead of picnicking out in the open, go inside and indulge yourselves with a meal under the table. This suggestion is sure to get a giggly response from your youngster. Simply put a sheet over the dinner table to make it into a tent and then move underneath to eat your picnic lunch or dinner.

Extensions:

- Darken the room and use a flashlight for the meal.
- Reverse the meal and have dessert first.

Abbreviate It

Time: 10 to 15 minutes

Materials: None

Teach the concept of abbreviating in a playful way. One of you thinks of two letters that the other has to turn into a phrase that matches the abbreviation. For example, FS could mean "feeling silly." Keep going as long as you can without getting stumped.

Extensions:

- Make up a list of abbreviations and write simple sentences that you take turns decoding.
- Save the list and send or deliver secret messages to each other that no one else will understand.

Backward Day

Time: All day

Materials: Common items used for self-care

Do your day backward. For example, you might begin the day with dinner, brush your teeth before you eat, put on your shoes before your shirt, or comb your hair and then mess it up.

Extensions:

- Eat dinner starting with dessert and working to the salad or first course.
- Have a burger and fries for breakfast, or an omelet for dinner.
- Wear some articles of your clothing backward.

Backward Drawing

Time: 15 to 20 minutes

Materials: Paper, pencil

Play around with a different way to draw by holding the pen still and moving the paper beneath it to make pictures and designs.

Extensions:

- Try simple drawings of objects.
- Try writing your names.

Birthday Encore

Time: 30 minutes

Materials: Pictures from magazines, poster board ($), colored felt pens ($)

Don't celebrate such a special day just once when you can make a bulletin board to highlight a birthday all month. Find wall space and create a paper border to outline it. Decorate the inside with things like the birth date, birthstone, astrological sign, birth flower, birthday traditions, favorite cake, and what your child liked best about that year.

Extensions:

- Add whatever your child wishes for in the coming year.
- Dig out photos from previous birthdays to see the growth that has taken place.
- Mark the half-year birthday and plan something special for that day.
- Mark a calendar with the birthdays of people who are special and think of ways to celebrate them.

Box Building

Time: 30 to 40 minutes

Materials: Boxes of all sizes, white glue, masking tape

Gather boxes of all sizes and check for and remove sharp staples. Work together to come up with a plan to cut, glue, and build something together.

Extensions:

- Add colored-paper scraps to make details and features.
- Create a city landscape with skyscrapers.
- Paint or color the boxes with felt pens ($).

Caveman Food

Time: 20 to 30 minutes

Materials: Dinner food items

Use your imaginations to plan a caveman meal. You might serve up a roast beef with whole baked potatoes along with a written menu dubbing your dinner dinosaur meat with whale eggs. Pea soup with fish crackers could become a drink from the lagoon. Let your imaginations be your guide.

Extension:

- Pretend you are giants and make up a menu like broccoli trees and carrot disks that are slices of logs.
- Draw pictures of your dishes to grace the mealtime table with visual effects.

Confetti Eggs

Time: 30 minutes

Materials: Sharp pin or needle, raw eggs, food coloring ($), paper confetti, clear tape, glue, small paintbrush ($)

You can crack open these colorful eggs and be showered with confetti. Method 1: Using the pin, poke a small hole in the end of an egg and blow out the insides. Save for cooking. The hole can be made as large as your middle finger is round. Color the egg using food coloring mixed in water and dry thoroughly. Use confetti to fill the egg as full as possible and tape over the opening. Method 2: Break the egg in half as you normally would. Dye and dry the egg and then fill the halves with confetti. Glue together with little pieces of colored tissue paper that are brushed on with glue. Eggs will release their contents when cracked.

Creamy Finger Paint

Time: 15 to 20 minutes

Materials: Can of shaving cream ($)

Finger painting was never easier, and your table will be spotless when you are done. Squirt several globs of shaving cream onto a table and finger paint with it, being careful to keep it away from the eyes.

Extensions:

- Add a few drops of scented flavorings, such as vanilla or lemon.
- Add some coconut ($) for a different feeling.
- Sprinkle the cream with a small amount of powdered tempera paint ($).

Copy Magic

Time: 30 minutes

Materials: White paper, crayons, ruler

This activity takes time, but if you do it together, it will go faster. Draw a picture or design with crayons on white paper, covering the white as much as possible with color. Small white spaces are fine. Place the paper colored-side down on top of a clean sheet of white paper the same size. Pull a ruler across the page several times, pressing down hard. The drawing will produce an exact duplicate on the sheet of paper that is below it.

Crazy Creatures

Time: 15 to 30 minutes

Materials: Package of 3 x 5–inch index cards ($), felt pens ($) or crayons

This activity takes a little time and precision but giggles are sure to result. Place three of the cards horizontally, one above the other, on a flat surface. Draw a head on the top card, a matching body on the middle card, and a set of legs and feet on the bottom card, trying to make all creatures about the same size as one another. Examples of creatures could include a robot, a duck with webbed feet, a princess, a clown, and a space creature. Repeat as many times as desired. Now the 3 piles of cards can each be shuffled and matched into crazy new creatures.

Extension:

- Exchange cards from the piles that each of you have made for even more variety.

Create an Ending

Time: 15 to 30 minutes

Materials: Storybook

You can take a favorite story and make it even better when you put your heads together. Read a good book and, when you finish, think of other good ways that the story could end.

Extensions:

- Talk about a favorite movie and make up new endings.
- Choose an ending to the story that you both like best, sharing why.

Cup of Fish

Time: 20 to 30 minutes

Materials: Clear cups or glasses, blue gelatin dessert mix ($), chewable gummy fish candies ($)

Gross snacks and mock bravado are a hit with school age children. Prepare the gelatin as directed on the package and put it in the refrigerator until partially set, about 1 hour. Place a few gummy fish in each cup and spoon in the gelatin. Return the mix to the refrigerator until it is fully set and ready to eat.

Extension:

- For a variation, freeze into popsicle molds or ice cubes.

Dinner Mix-Up

Time: 15 to 20 minutes

Materials: Thin cardboard, pencil

Family members are used to coming to the dinner table every night and sitting in the same place. Cut the cardboard into pieces that can be folded over to stand. Then, shake things up by making name place cards and arranging where people will sit, making sure that everyone is in a seat that is not his or her usual spot.

Extensions:

- Number each seat and have people roll dice to determine which seat to take.
- Arrange people alphabetically by first name.
- Work together to think of new ways to assign seating at the table.

Dinosaur Trap

Time: 45 minutes to 1 hour

Materials: Large piece of cardboard, glue, tape, scraps of odds and ends such as egg cartons, milk cartons, wood scraps, coat hangers, film canisters, spools, boxes, etc., small plastic dinosaur ($)

This is an imaginative project that will take planning and collaboration. Study the materials together to come up with a design for a dinosaur trap, talking about how it would work.

Extensions:

- Design traps for other creatures, real or imaginary.
- Make a house to keep the dinosaur in after it is captured.
- Do some research and plan a menu for what it will eat.

Edible Jewelry

Time: 20 to 30 minutes

Materials: Food items that can be strung, like black licorice shoestring, cereal pieces with holes, Lifesaver candies, and knotted pretzels ($)

Measure the licorice and cut it in lengths for bracelets and necklaces making sure to allow enough length to tie a knot. String on the other candies, cereal, and pretzels and wear until you get hungry.

Extensions:

- Wrap the jewelry items and give them as gifts.
- Cover a small box with the items, using a glue of confectioners' sugar ($) thinned with water to make an edible house with windows and doors.
- Use the same glue as above ($) to stick items to a strip of cardboard that can be held in the hand or kept in the car for a snack. Package in sealable plastic bags ($).

Giant Hats

Time: 20 to 30 minutes

Materials: Paper grocery bag; scissors; glue or tape; decorative items like feathers, yarn, sequins, glitter, buttons, bits of paper, or ribbon ($); crayons or markers

Draw 2 large cone hat shapes and cut them out. Tape the edges together, checking for the fit, and then decorate both sides by gluing or taping on the other items.

Extensions:

- Use extra strips of paper bags to make hair by cutting it in fringes and stapling it on.
- Make a crown or other theme hat.

Goop

Time: 20 minutes

Materials: 2 cups salt, 1 cup water, 1 cup of cornstarch ($), container with lid or sealable plastic bag ($)

You've never felt anything quite like Goop! Cook the salt and ½ cup of water for 4 to 5 minutes over medium heat. Remove from heat and add the cornstarch and the remaining water. Return to the heat and stir until the mixture thickens. Store it in a tight container or sealable plastic bag.

Extensions:

- Add food coloring to the mixture.
- Use while warm or heat the Goop gently in the microwave.
- Add cooking extract or a squirt of cologne to the Goop.
- Go outdoors and feel the Goop in a plastic tub with your bare feet.

Homemade Stickers

Time: 20 to 30 minutes

Materials: White paper, ruler, pencil, ½ tsp. of sugar, markers or crayons, package of unflavored gelatin ($), small paintbrush ($), water

You can turn anything into a sticker using this easy recipe. Use the ruler and pencil to divide the paper into same-sized areas that will become the actual stickers. Color designs or pictures onto each square. Mix the adhesive* as outlined below, and brush it onto the back side of the paper. The page will curl up, but when it is completely dry, it can be pressed flat with a heavy phone book. Cut into individual stickers and lick to apply.

*Adhesive: Sprinkle 1 packet of unflavored gelatin into a small bowl with 1 tablespoon of cold water. Let soften for 5 minutes. Add 3 tablespoons of boiling water and stir until dissolved. Add ½ teaspoon of sugar.

Extensions:

- Use small pictures cut from magazines to make into stickers.
- Add a few drops of flavored extract ($), such as peppermint or lemon, to the glue for a better taste.

Jewelry Dough

Time: 30 to 40 minutes

Materials: ¾ cup flour, ½ cup salt, ½ cup cornstarch, warm water, string, toothpick, poster paint ($)

This is a good activity to do over several days. Mix the flour, salt, cornstarch, and warm water well until it can be kneaded into shapes. Make beads by rolling the dough into little balls and piercing the centers with a toothpick. Allow the beads to dry overnight. Paint them with poster paints and string them into jewelry.

Extensions:

- Glue beads together into a free-form sculpture.
- Flatten the bottoms to use as game pieces in a homemade game.
- Mold the dough into snowman and Santa shapes to make ornaments. Remember to insert a tree hook into the headpieces before drying.

Negative Space

Time: 20 minutes

Materials: Paper, crayons or pencils, water colors ($)

There is no telling what you will end up with when you create using negative space. Paint an irregular shape on a piece of paper using water colors. Let dry. Make a drawing that uses the painted space as part of the picture.

Extension:

- Make 2 or more painted shapes on the paper.

New Rules

Time: 15 to 30 minutes

Materials: Any familiar table board game ($)

Bring out your favorite game and turn it into a whole new adventure by changing one rule. For example, remove half of the checkers or game pieces or one of the dice.

Extension:

- Make up a new game by suggesting and agreeing on several new rules. Talk about what happened when the game is finished.

Pet Egg

Time: 30 minutes

Materials: Empty eggshell with the top removed about ⅓ of the way down, empty paper-towel roll, markers, cotton balls, alfalfa seed ($)

This little pet grows a full head of hair in a matter of days. Rinse out the eggshell and place it open-side up in a holder cut from an empty paper-towel roll. Draw a face on the eggshell using colored markers. Put 3 damp cotton balls in the shell and sprinkle with alfalfa seeds. Keep the cotton damp for the next 2 or 3 days until the seeds begin to sprout. Put in a sunny spot and as the sprouts grow, and you will have a live head of hair growing above the face.

Extensions:

- Give the egg friend a green face and call it a leprechaun.
- Give the egg creature a haircut and watch it grow back in a few days.

Rainbow Craft Noodles

Time: 30 minutes

Materials: Paper towels, 1 pound of dry noodles shaped like tubes or wheels ($), rubbing alcohol, food coloring ($), containers

Pasta never had it so good! Noodles are great for a variety of crafts from necklaces to collages and colored noodles are even more fun. Make your own supply by putting the noodles in a large container (a separate one for each color) so that there is plenty of room for the alcohol. Add alcohol and food coloring, and make sure all of the noodles are covered in the mixture. Let stand as long as you wish, using a lengthier time for deeper and brighter colors. Place the noodles on paper towels to dry for at least a few hours. These are perfect for making jewelry, collages, or sculptures.

Sand Art

Time: 20 to 30 minutes

Materials: Paper, white glue, sand ($)

This activity requires a little practice to get the idea, but the unique feeling makes it well worth the time. Write a message or draw a picture on paper using glue. Try to avoid globs of glue and be sure to leave the paper flat on the table while working. Before the glue dries, sprinkle lightly with dry sand. Allow the work to remain unmoved for at least half an hour and then shake off the excess sand.

Extensions:

- For variety, use colored sand ($) from a hobby store.
- Use colored glue that you make yourself by adding food coloring ($).

Sand Casting

Time: 40 minutes to 1 hour

Materials: Empty coffee can, cold water, sandbox or several pans full of sand ($), plaster of paris mix ($), hook for wall-hanging (optional) ($)

Your child will love mixing this new medium and seeing the amazing results when it sets. Dig an irregular impression in the sand an inch or two deep and as big as you want the final product to be. If you poke a few holes with your finger, the casting will have bumps. Mix the plaster in an old coffee can by pouring about 2 cups of cold water and enough of the plaster mix to bring it to the consistency of a milkshake. Spoon it into the impression to a thickness of about an inch and a half. (A hook can be inserted for a wall hanging if you wish.) Let set for 45 minutes to an hour and lift out carefully with both hands. Brush away the excess sand.

Extensions:

- Put a few shells, stones, and twigs into the impression before adding the plaster.
- Use white glue to add a small photograph when finished.

Scribble Art

Time: 15 to 20 minutes

Materials: Paper, pencils

This activity takes both of you to make it work. Take turns making a simple scribble in the middle of a piece of paper for the other to turn into something recognizable by incorporating the scribble into a new picture. If one of you gets stumped, work together to come up with an answer.

Extension:

- Work together to make 2 simple scribbles on the same page to turn into a picture.

Sidewalk-Art Contest

Time: 40 minutes to 1 hour

Materials: Paper, colored chalk ($)

Art is fun together, but you can take it a step further by inviting the neighborhood gang to join a sidewalk-art contest. Agree on the time and place, and make up a list of categories and prizes (perhaps ice cream or other cool treats). Make sure that everyone wins, even if you have to invent additional categories to make that happen.

Extensions:

- Take photos of the entries and give them to the artists.
- Have a clean-up party several days later at an agreed-upon time, when everyone can throw buckets of water on the drawings to conclude the event.

Silly News Flash

Time: 10 to 15 minutes

Materials: None

When you're feeling silly, this one will keep the mood going. Sit in a comfortable position and begin a news story using only 3 words. The next person adds 3 more words, and this continues until the news story is complete. An example might be something like, "Early this morning, a pink elephant, walked upstairs loudly...etc."

Extensions:

- Change the rules in a mutually agreeable way, such as alternating complete sentences or changing the number of allowed words.
- Write down the stories and read them back later for more laughs.

Smooth Writing

Time: 20 to 30 minutes

Materials: Paper, liquid starch ($), colored chalk ($)

You and your child will enjoy the slippery fun of this unusual art project. Pour a small amount of starch on the paper and spread it evenly over the surface with your hands. Rinse your hands and then draw with the chalk on the slippery surface. Allow the drawing to dry thoroughly before moving it.

Extensions:

- Do the same activity with slow and then fast music. Decide if the different tempos made a difference.
- Use primary colors of chalk that will blend to make a new color, such as red and yellow to make orange or blue and yellow to make green.

Snow Globe

Time: 30 minutes

Materials: Small glass jars with lids, glue, small plastic toys, white corn syrup ($), glitter ($)

The fascination of a snow globe can be yours for pennies. Glue a small toy or figurine upright inside the jar lid, making sure that the entire toy will fit into the jar when it is inserted and closed. Let it dry for at least 2 hours. Fill the jar with white corn syrup, leaving a small gap at the top. Add some glitter for the snow. Glue the lid to the jar and allow it to dry for 15 to 20 minutes. Shake to make a blizzard. These are perfect for inexpensive holiday and birthday gifts.

Spooky Surprise Box

Time: 15 to 30 minutes

Materials: Medium-sized box, glitter and paint ($), warm grapes, wet spaghetti, small twigs, gelatin ($), plastic spiders and bugs ($), yarn or imitation cobweb ($)

Spooky fun is perfect for children of this age. Cut a hole in the side of the box about 2 to 3 inches round and another hole on the opposite end about 4 or 5 inches round. Decorate the outside of the box. One person puts his hand through the smaller hole and another person passes him an object to feel without looking, mentioning that they are passing skeleton bones (sticks), eyeballs (warm grapes), brains (wet spaghetti), or guts (gelatin warmed to room temperature).

Stained Glass

Time: 30 minutes

Materials: Knife; scissors; an iron; flat objects like dried leaves, paper scraps, or magazine pictures; wax paper ($); crayons

This is a fun activity that requires your close participation and supervision, reserving knife and ironing tasks for yourself. Arrange the flat objects on a sheet of wax paper and add crayon shavings for color accents (use the knife to shave the crayons). Add a second layer of wax paper on the top and cover with a few more layers of wax paper. Iron the assembled packet on medium heat, checking frequently to avoid burning. Stop when the paper is stuck together and the crayons are melted. Cool and trim off the edges.

Extensions:

- Cut into shapes and hang on a window like stained glass.
- Make greeting cards or bookmarks by folding a sheet of paper in half and cutting a rectangle out of the folded side. Mount the stained glass behind paper using tape.

Tall Tales

Time: 5 to 10 minutes

Materials: Shoe box, small common household objects

The more people that play this game, the more fun it is. Fill the box with small items and take turns selecting an item and making up a story about it. For example, if a key were selected, you could come up with something like, "This key saved the life of a man who had it in his pocket next to his heart when he was shot by a fleeing bank robber." Continue making up the silliest stories you can think of.

Extensions:

- Take a walk or a bike ride and make up similar stories with things that you see along the way.
- Keep a list of the best story lines and enjoy them from time to time.
- Have a family contest and make awards for the tallest tales.

Wrap It Up

Time: 20 to 30 minutes

Materials: Fabric scraps, scissors, string or yarn ($)

Let your imaginations run wild as you make whimsical costumes together. Collect all of the fabric scraps that you can and spread out in an area with lots of elbowroom, placing all the material in the center. Begin with one body part and decorate it by using the materials. Consider making cone heads, over-sized muscular arms, huge clown feet, or bulging stomachs. Be sure to have a camera on hand.

Extensions:

- Provide needles and thread to make the costumes sturdier and more permanent.
- Use a stapler or duct tape to hold creations together more easily.

Places to Go

Creating memories with children means taking them to places where you can have fun and create memories together. In the diapers and naps stage, outings are necessarily short, but when children reach the preschool years, the possibilities become endless. Consider the following guidelines before you head out and you can eliminate many of the problems that can get in the way of the good times you want to have together:

- You don't need to spend a fortune to enjoy your time together. There are many free and low-cost options available that young children will enjoy. In the listings below,
  - $ denotes free or low cost
  - $$ denotes moderate cost
  - $$$ means that you may need to budget for this activity in advance
- Preplanning is essential for any outing, even the shortest, so you can conveniently meet needs for toileting, eating, thirst, and weather conditions. Carry water and snacks wherever you go and find out where restrooms are ahead of time or as soon as you arrive at your destination.

- Remember that being in a new environment is highly stimulating, and young children are apt to tune you out as their eyes bounce from one new thing to the next. Be extra vigilant for their safety in crowds, while crossing streets and parking lots, and when looking at machinery or exhibits.

Camping: $

If this is an activity that you enjoy, so will your children. Be sure to include them in the campsite chores and end the day with the fun of singing around a campfire drinking steamy cocoa. If you are new to camping but would like to give it a try, contact local outdoors organizations like the Sierra Club for a safe and well-planned experience.

Playgrounds: $

The only cost associated here might be stopping for a treat along the way. Check out local parks and find those with the most up-to-date equipment, as safety standards have been upgraded over the past 10 years in many states. Fast-food playgrounds are appealing to children, but if you go there, high-fat foods will become a strong temptation.

Picnics: $

Rare is the child who will not jump at the chance to go on a picnic. Picnics mean eating with the fingers while taking in the outdoors. On the spur of the moment, try the back lawn, a local park, or pull off on a country road. Children can also help to plan the menu and pack the food, which will make it taste even better to them.

Community Events: $

Check your local newspaper for listings of special events in your community. Many of them are designed specifically for families and are free or low cost. Seasonal, multicultural, and holiday events can be found in every town, and if you mark your calendar, you will have a reminder to repeat the fun next year.

Park-District Classes and Events: $

Local park districts offer a variety of low-cost classes for children, particularly during holiday and summer vacations. Your child might learn to dance, bake treats, or create an artistic masterpiece. End with a picnic and you'll have a lovely day together.

Transportation: $

If you have a local transit system, head off on a bus or ferry for a new adventure and a different view of your city. Check times and have the correct change available to minimize delays.

Nature Walks: $

An outing that never fails is a walk around the neighborhood, and if you make it a point, you can find something new every time. Walking together also gives you a chance to talk and share feelings and ideas and to collect interesting pieces of this and that along the way. It is also a way to model and build healthy exercise habits.

Farms: $

Not many children get to see where their food comes from, so a trip to a farm where you can pick produce will be interesting and exciting. Prices are generally reduced at picking farms, and you can go home and bake a treat afterward to share.

Art Galleries: $

In limited doses, many children enjoy viewing and talking about art. Some art museums even have sections designed just for children. Stick to a room or two and intersperse it with a juice break at the museum cafe. When your child begins to whine or fidget, it's time to leave.

Farmer's Markets: $

Open-air markets of fresh produce are enjoying renewed popularity across the country, and much of the produce is organic and pesticide free. Entertainment and music are often included, and you can take home something healthy to make for a snack or meal.

Factories: $

Local factories make fascinating destinations, and if the product is candy or ice cream, it can be like a fairy tale. Newspapers also make a good choice, as the papers spill off the presses at top speed.

Movies: $$

Always a special outing, this one can rise in cost when goodies are included, and you may want to call ahead to check prices. Matinees offer substantial savings if your schedule permits, but snack prices are not usually reduced. Special caution should be exercised when selecting a film, being careful not to cave in to pressure from your child to see an inappropriate film that the media is pushing through targeted advertising.

Amusement Parks: $$

For children ages 5 through 8, a trip to an amusement park can be the highlight of a summer vacation. Be prepared for lots of walking, and carry water if it is a hot day. Children usually know their own limits, and some are more daredevil than others. Follow their pace and the day will go well.

Vacation Travel: $$$

Family trips require planning and budgeting, with lifelong memories as the reward. Automobile associations and travel agencies can offer you good advice on destinations and what you should take along. Preparation is half the fun, so take time to read together about what you will see and where you will go. It is wise to determine the amount of souvenir money available for the whole trip before you leave and to use this as a chance to experience budgeting and decision making.

Stocking the Toy Shelf

Having the right playthings on hand can go a long way toward assuring that developmental targets are met and that there is enough on hand to keep children happily engaged; however, you may also want to consider the following Do's and Don'ts for making playtime as smooth as possible.

Buying Do's

- Look for sturdy toys such as stitched dolls, wooden blocks, and puzzles with heavy pieces.
- Provide play and playthings that offer new experiences.
- Store toys where your child can get to them easily and without help.
- Keep parts stored together (an end of the day task) so you don't lose any parts.
- Consider if you are buying something that will require special care or arrangements.
- Keep safety in mind. A good rule of thumb for children ages 3 and under is to avoid anything that can fit through a toilet-paper tube.
- Tell your child why you selected a particular gift/toy.
- Make children responsible for cleaning up after play, helping them so it becomes part of the play.

- Remember that paying a lot for a toy doesn't mean you will get high play-value.
- Suggested ages on toy boxes are fairly reliable, and buying something more advanced will not speed up that timetable.
- Consider toys that require pretend play and imagination such as hats, dish sets, children's tools, and dolls.

Buying Don'ts

- Avoid overwhelming a child with more than one or two new gifts/toys at a time.
- Never make comparisons to other family members' gifts.
- Toy boxes encourage dumping and lost pieces.

Playthings from around the House

Infants

- People and lots of attention
- Common household items to look at and listen to

Toddlers

- Cans
- Large spoons and spatulas
- Kitchen pots and lids
- Milk and egg cartons
- Shoes
- Bright scarves
- Empty boxes
- Purses to empty and fill

Ages Three and Four

- Books with large pictures
- Kitchen utensils for water and dirt play
- Hats
- Shoes
- Old clothing
- Pencils and pens

- Sponges
- Vegetable brushes
- Cards
- Large boxes to crawl through
- Pouring and measuring tools
- Real hammers with large-head nails

Kindergarten through Grade 3

- Jars to collect insects
- Mud, sand, and water
- Junk jewelry for pretend play
- Cards
- Flashlight
- Garden tools
- Wheelbarrow
- Paper punch
- Large needle, thread, and fabric

Worthwhile Things to Buy

If you want to purchase toys or to give a gift to your child, the following suggestions can help to assure that your purchases will be appropriate, long lasting, and fun:

Babies

- Soft, squeezable animals and dolls
- Mobile
- Music box
- Basket of baby books
- Soft ball
- Spinning top

Toddlers

- Child-sized table and chair
- Doll bottle
- Finger puppets

- Toy mop and broom
- Nesting cups
- Push-and-pull toys
- Rhythm instruments
- Balls of various sizes
- Soft plastic toys
- Soft dolls without buttons or eyes
- Sturdy books
- Plastic keys
- Play telephone
- Music boxes
- Toy camera
- Broomstick horse
- Step stool
- Playhouse

Ages Three and Four

- Picture storybooks
- Balls
- Dolls
- Art supplies
- Small garden tools
- Plastic tea and cooking sets
- Three-wheel riding toys
- Wagon
- Cars
- Wooden unit blocks
- Plastic lunch box
- Toy telephone
- 20- to 30-piece puzzles
- Electric toothbrush
- Trucks for dumping sand and dirt

Kindergarten through Grade 3

- Backpack
- Kites
- Butterfly net
- Jump rope
- Tape recorder
- Two-wheel bicycle and safty helmet
- Lunch box
- Board games
- Skates
- Yo-yo
- Gyroscope
- Picture dictionary
- Puzzles of the USA and the world
- Tap shoes
- Easel
- Art supplies
- Play kitchen
- Tool bench
- Cars and trucks
- Lego table
- Brio train
- Doctor kit
- Ant farm
- Bird feeder
- Croquet set
- Frisbee
- Construction sets

Index

About the Author

Susan Kettmann, M.S.Ed., is a Child Development Specialist residing in San Francisco, California, with more than twenty years of experience working with children and families in education and government settings. Long holding a special interest in the effect of appropriate adult-child interactions on positive skills development, she collected the many activities in this book during those years. Ms. Kettmann also taught Child Development classes to parents and preschool teachers at the community college level for fifteen years. She currently works for the Marin County Health and Human Services Department and spends much of her free time playing with her three grandchildren.